Enhancing the Search Experience in SharePoint 2013

STEVEN MANN

Cover By: David H. Ross (http://davidhross.com/)

Table of Contents

This page intentionally blank

Introduction

This book provides many ideas and steps for enhancing the search experience across various aspects of SharePoint 2013 Enterprise Search. Enterprise Search in SharePoint 2013 Server provides an abundance of functionality and search capabilities for your SharePoint environment. There are many ways to enhance the overall search experience for your users by customizing the search features, templates, and settings.

I hope you find this book useful and if you have any questions or other twists that I do not address, please send me an email (steve@stevethemanmann.com) and I will be glad to assist you.

Stay updated with my blog posts: www.SteveTheManMann.com

Reference links and source code is available on www.stevethemanmann.com:

This page intentionally blank

CHAPTER 1

Enhancing the Search Box UX

This chapter walks you through the various options and settings available for the Search Box web part.

Adding the Verticals Drop Down to the Search Box

Before the results pages are modified, the main page of the Search Center may be tweaked by modifying the Search Box web part on that page.

Navigate to your Search Center:

From the Settings menu, select Edit Page:

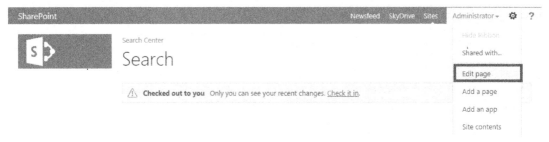

The page is presented in edit mode and is checked out to you automatically.

Click on Edit Web Part from the Search Box drop-down menu:

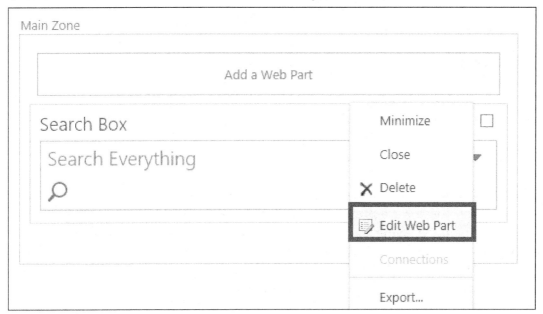

The Search Box Properties pane appears to the right of the page.

Select the Turn on drop-down Search Navigation option and click OK:

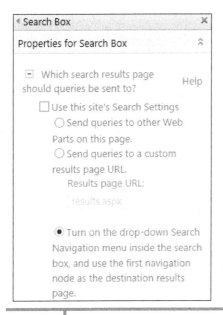

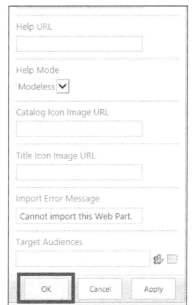

Check in the page:

 Checked out to you Only you can see your recent changes. Check it in. ⬅

Publish the page:

 Recent draft not published Visitors can't see recent changes. Publish this draft. ⬅

Now the user has an option to search within a defined context and navigate directly to that results page. These were previously named "scopes". Clicking Enter or clicking on the search button (magnifying glass) sends the query to the Everything page (re-sults.aspx).

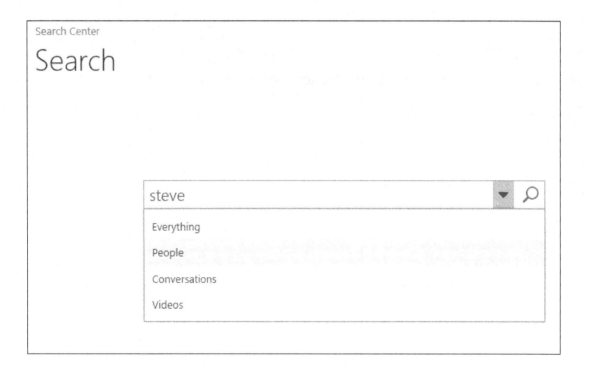

Displaying Links Next to the Search Box

You may modify the Search Box web part properties to display certain links next to the
search box:

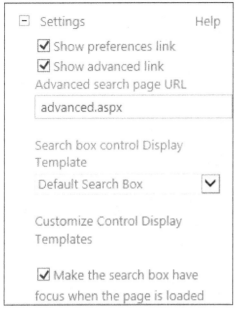

The Show preferences link option displays a link next to the Search Box where users may
modify their search experience. The Show advanced link also displays a link to the right
of the Search Box and navigates the user to the advanced search page.

Setting Focus on the Search Box

In the Settings section of the Search Box web part properties, there is an option to set the focus behavior:

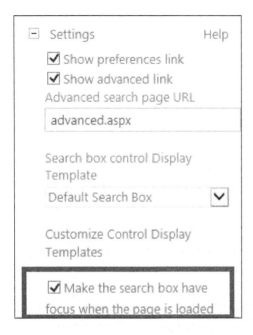

The **Make the search box have focus when the page is loaded** option places the cursor inside the search box so the user does not have to click inside to make a change.

Adding Suggestions to the Search Box

Suggestions Overview

bike|	$\mathcal{O}$
Bike Wash - Dissolver	
All-Purpose **Bike** Stand	
Hitch Rack - 4-**Bike**	
Mountain **Bike** Socks, L	
Mountain **Bike** Socks, M	

Suggestions are words or phrases that appear automatically when a user is typing search terms into a search box. Suggestions are enabled by default in both the Search Service Application and the Search Box web parts.

SharePoint automatically adds terms to the internal suggestion list based on user search actions. Once a term has been searched/queried and a result clicked a total of six (6) times, that term becomes part of the suggestion list.

This allows the suggestions to grow organically within your organization based on user past user search experiences. However, you may also add a list of suggestions to Share-Point to use. The sections to follow show you how to do just that.

When you add a list of suggestions to the Search Service Application, all previous suggestions are removed. Therefore, it is a good idea to start off with a suggestion list before going live with your new Search Center.

Create a Suggestion File

A suggestion file is just a text file that contains a word or phrase on each line. It may be anything that you feel will help your user search content. Some ideas include listing out products, clients/customers, contacts, etc. and using those values in the suggestion text file. For example purposes, I am going to list out all of the product names from the end-to-end bonus chapters:

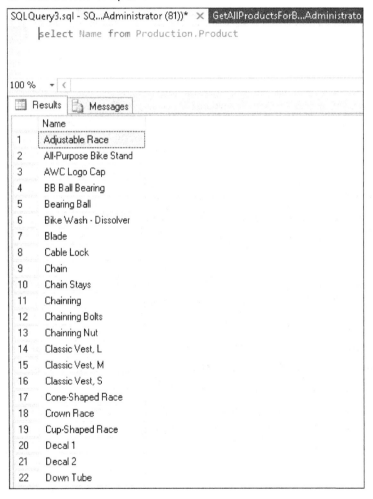

Copy and paste the list into a text file:

```
Suggestions.txt - Notepad
File  Edit  Format  View  Help
Adjustable Race
All-Purpose Bike Stand
AWC Logo Cap
BB Ball Bearing
Bearing Ball
Bike Wash - Dissolver
Blade
Cable Lock
Chain
Chain Stays
Chainring
Chainring Bolts
Chainring Nut
Classic Vest, L
Classic Vest, M
Classic Vest, S
Cone-Shaped Race
Crown Race
Cup-Shaped Race
Decal 1
Decal 2
Down Tube
External Lock Washer 1
External Lock Washer 2
External Lock Washer 3
External Lock Washer 4
External Lock Washer 5
External Lock Washer 6
External Lock Washer 7
External Lock Washer 8
External Lock Washer 9
Fender Set - Mountain
Flat Washer 1
Flat Washer 2
Flat Washer 3
Flat Washer 4
Flat Washer 5
Flat Washer 6
Flat Washer 7
```

Save the text file and get ready for import.

Import the Suggestion File

To import a suggestion file, navigate to your Search Service Application and click on Query Suggestions under the Queries and Results section of the left-hand navigation:

Queries and Results
Authoritative Pages
Result Sources
Query Rules
Query Client Types
Search Schema
Query Suggestions
Search Dictionaries
Search Result Removal

Click on the Import from text file link on the Query Suggestion Settings page:

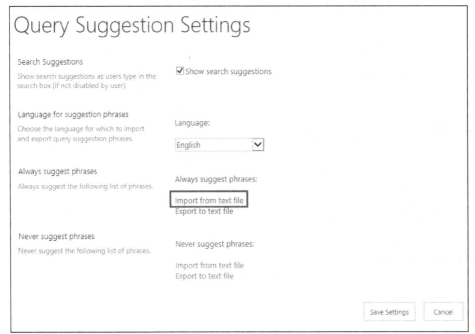

Query Suggestion Settings

Search Suggestions

Show search suggestions as users type in the search box (if not disabled by user).

☑ Show search suggestions

Language for suggestion phrases

Choose the language for which to import and export query suggestion phrases.

Language:

English ⌄

Always suggest phrases

Always suggest the following list of phrases.

Always suggest phrases:

Import from text file
Export to text file

Never suggest phrases

Never suggest the following list of phrases.

Never suggest phrases:

Import from text file
Export to text file

Save Settings   Cancel

Click the Browse button to locate and select your suggestion text file:

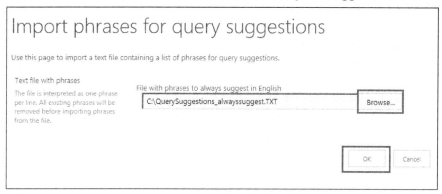

Click OK.

For good measure, click Save Settings:

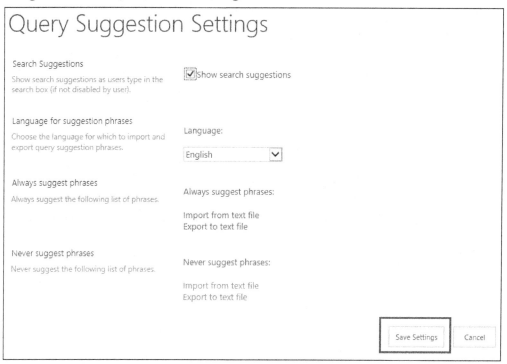

Process Query Suggestions

After the suggestions are imported, they will not appear until they are processed. They are processed via a timer job in SharePoint.

So instead of holding your breath to see the suggestions work, navigate to Central Administration and click on Monitoring from the left-hand navigation:

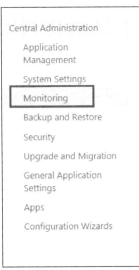

Click on Review job definitions under Timer Jobs:

On the Job Definitions page, scroll down to the bottom and click the arrow to go to the next page:

1-100 ▸

Scroll up on the next page and click on the Prepare Query Suggestions:

Title

My Site Instantiation Interactive Request Queue

My Site Instantiation Non-Interactive Request Queue

My Site Instantiation Non-Interactive Request Queue

My Site Second Instantiation Interactive Request Queue

My Site Second Instantiation Interactive Request Queue

Notification Timer Job c02c63c2-12d8-4ec0-b678-f05c7e00570e

Notification Timer Job c02c63c2-12d8-4ec0-b678-f05c7e00570e

Password Management

Performance Metric Provider

Persisted Navigation Term Set Synchronization

Persisted Navigation Term Set Synchronization

Prepare query suggestions

Product Version Job

Query Classification Dictionary Update for Search Application Search Service Application.

Query Logging

Rebalance crawl store partitions for Search Service Application

On the Edit Timer Job page, click Run Now:

Job Description

Prepares candidate queries for query suggestion and performs pre-computations for result block ranking.

Job Properties

This section lists the properties for this job.

Web application: N/A

Last run time: 4/19/2013 5:43 PM

Recurring Schedule

Use this section to modify the schedule specifying when the timer job will run. Daily, weekly, and monthly schedules also include a window of execution. The timer service will pick a random time within this interval to begin executing the job on each applicable server. This feature is appropriate for high-load jobs which run on multiple servers on the farm. Running this type of job on all the servers simultaneously might place an unreasonable load on the farm. To specify an exact starting time, set the beginning and ending times of the interval to the same value.

This timer job is scheduled to run:

○ Minutes   Starting every day between
○ Hourly   [1 AM ▾] [00 ▾]
◉ Daily   and no later than
○ Weekly   [11 PM ▾] [30 ▾]
○ Monthly

[Run Now]   [Disable]   [OK]   [Cancel]

The time job runs fairly quickly. You may view the results as explained in the next section.

View Suggestion Results

Navigate to your Search Center and type in a few letters that match some of your suggestion words/phrases:

The matching suggestions appear under the Search Box. You may modify the suggestion behavior as explained in the next section.

Configuring Suggestions in the Search Box Web Part

By default the Search Box is set to show suggestions. You may also elect to show people name suggestions. This provides functionality similar to an auto-complete. You may configure how many suggestions appear and how long it takes to show suggestions based on the number of minimum characters configured.

```
☐ Query Suggestions          Help

    ☑ Show suggestions
    ☐ Show people name
    suggestions

    Number of query suggestions
    ┌──────────────────────────┐
    │ 5                        │
    └──────────────────────────┘

    Minimum number of characters
    ┌──────────────────────────┐
    │ 2                        │
    └──────────────────────────┘

    Suggestions delay (in
    milliseconds)
    ┌──────────────────────────┐
    │ 100                      │
    └──────────────────────────┘

    ☑ Show personal favorite results
    Number of personal favorites
    ┌──────────────────────────┐
    │ 3                        │
    └──────────────────────────┘
```

The Search Box web part on each results page in your Search Center may be modified to change the behavior of suggestions and thus modify the user experience.

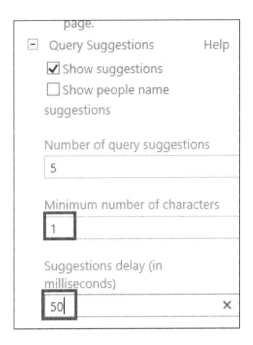

I like changing the minimum characters to 1 and the suggestions delay to 50 milliseconds. This allows the suggestions to appear quicker.

THIS PAGE INTENTIONALLY BLANK

CHAPTER 2

Enhancing the Search Navigation

This chapter walks through modifying and configuring the Search Navigation.

Accessing the Search Navigation Configuration Page

Navigate to your Search Center and select Site Settings from the Settings menu:

Under the Search section, click on Search Settings:

The Search Settings page appears:

The Search Navigation configuration is facilitated at the bottom of the page. Scroll down and continue to the next section of this guide for the configuration steps.

Configuring the Search Navigation

The Search Navigation configuration is located at the bottom of the Search Settings page for the current Site:

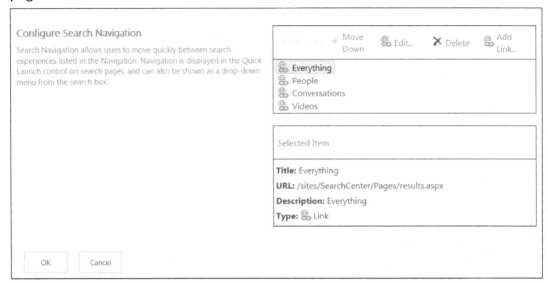

Click on Add Link...

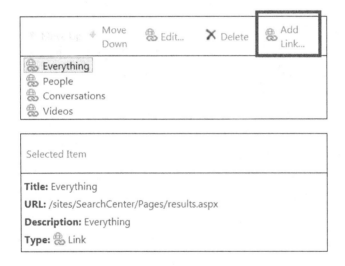

The Navigation Link dialog appears.

Enter Reports as the title and /sites/SearchCenter/Pages/reportsanddataresults.aspx as the URL:

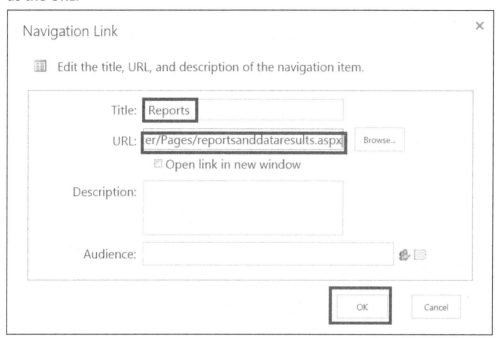

Click OK.

The Reports navigation link is added:

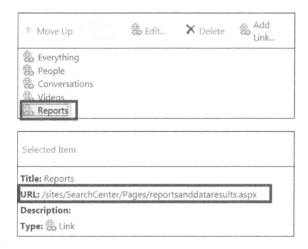

To demonstrate the Search Navigation Web Part overflow handling, you'll add another link.

Click on Add Link.. again:

The Navigation Link dialog appears again.

Enter Advanced as the title, /sites/SearchCenter/Pages/advanced.aspx as the URL, and click OK:

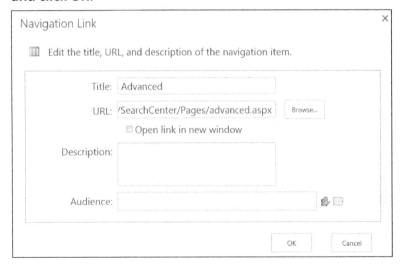

The Advanced navigation link is created:

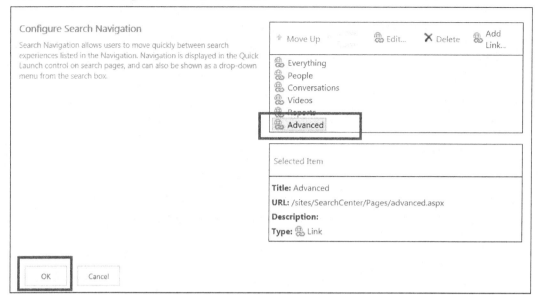

Click OK.

Return to your Search Center and perform a search.

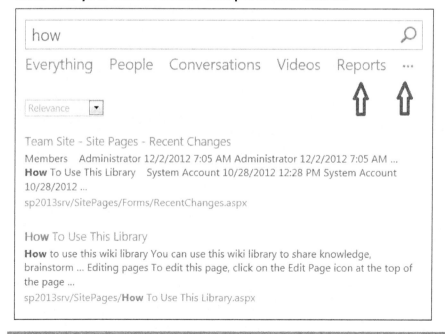

The Reports navigation displays but there are an ellipsis for the Advanced:

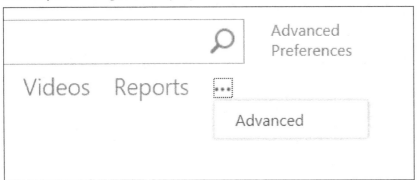

This is based on the setting in the Search Navigation web part. If you edit the page and edit the Search Navigation web part, you can change this as explained in the next section.

Modifying the Search Navigation Web Part

You do not modify the Search Navigation web part to modify the actual search navigation. You simply modify the web part to alter the display of the search navigation pages.

Navigate to a results page and use the Settings menu to edit the page:

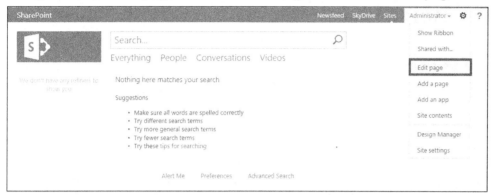

Select Edit Web Part from the Search Navigation drop-down menu:

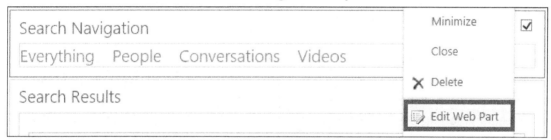

The Search Navigation web part properties are displayed on the right:

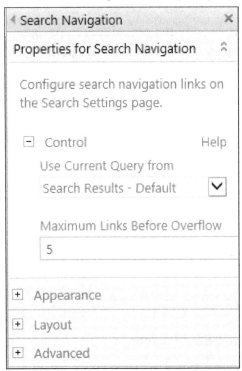

Essentially, the main setting here is the Maximum Links Before Overflow. As you add more pages to your navigation, the web part may not display all of them. Instead the web part displays an ellipsis ("...") that the user may click to see the additional navigation pages. I personally do not like this functionality so I usually set the maximum links to at least the amount of navigation pages I have.

Change the Maximum Links Before Overflow value to 6 and click OK:

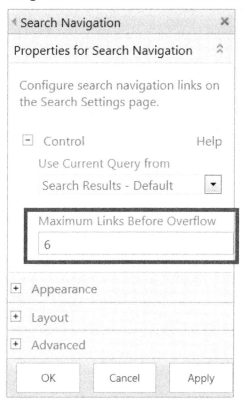

Now all of the search navigation links are displayed without an ellipsis:

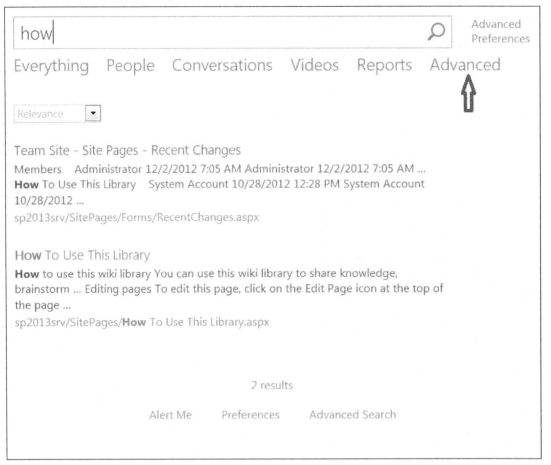

The end-to-end bonus chapters involve adding new results pages and including them within the navigation.

NOTE: Although the navigation flows through to all search results pages within the site, the overflow setting does not. Therefore, you need to modify the Search Navigation web part on each search result page within your Search Center site.

CHAPTER 3

Enhancing Search Results UX

Modifying the Search Results Web Part Settings

Navigate to a results page and use the Settings menu to edit the page:

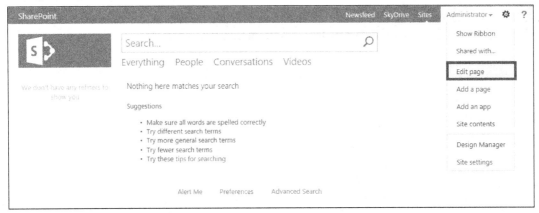

Select Edit Web Part from the Search Results drop-down menu:

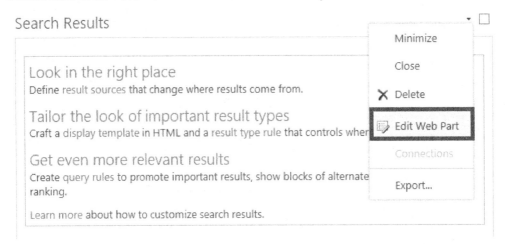

The Search Results web part properties pane is displayed on the right of the page:

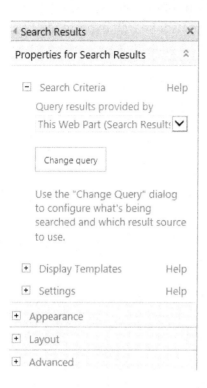

The Search Criteria and Display Templates are covered in more advanced chapters of this book. For the main search results, these should not be modified anyway. However, the Settings section provides several options to enhance the user search experience.

Expand the Settings section:

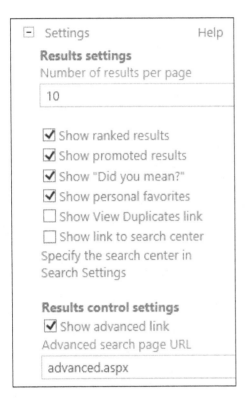

The default number of results is 10. I usually increase this to maximum of 50. I keep the next few settings as is to show various options. You do not need to show the link to the search center since you are already in the Search Center. This option is for Search Results that may be on another site.

The Show advanced link is similar to the Search Box web part but determines if the Advanced link is shown at the bottom of the results:

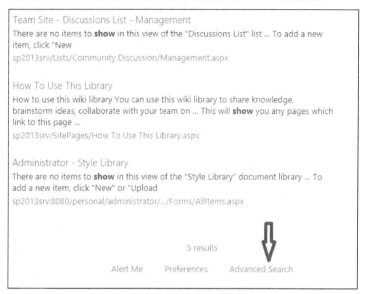

Scroll down for more settings:

The Show result count option determines if the result count is displayed in the search results:

Team Site - Discussions List - Management

There are no items to **show** in this view of the "Discussions List" list ... To add a new item, click "New

sp2013srv/Lists/Community Discussion/Management.aspx

How To Use This Library

How to use this wiki library You can use this wiki library to share knowledge, brainstorm ideas, collaborate with your team on ... This will **show** you any pages which link to this page ...

sp2013srv/SitePages/How To Use This Library.aspx

Administrator - Style Library

There are no items to **show** in this view of the "Style Library" document library ... To add a new item, click "New" or "Upload

sp2013srv:8080/personal/administrator/.../Forms/AllItems.aspx

5 results

Alert Me   Preferences   Advanced Search

(Sorting is explained in the next section)

The Show paging option allows users to go to the next page of results. I usually keep this checked. The Show preferences link option determines if the Preferences link is displayed within the Search Results:

Team Site - Discussions List - Management
There are no items to **show** in this view of the "Discussions List" list ... To add a new item, click "New
sp2013srv/Lists/Community Discussion/Management.aspx

How To Use This Library
How to use this wiki library You can use this wiki library to share knowledge, brainstorm ideas, collaborate with your team on ... This will **show** you any pages which link to this page ...
sp2013srv/SitePages/How To Use This Library.aspx

Administrator - Style Library
There are no items to **show** in this view of the "Style Library" document library ... To add a new item, click "New" or "Upload
sp2013srv:8080/personal/administrator/.../Forms/AllItems.aspx

 5 results

Alert Me   Preferences   Advanced Search

The Show alertme link option determines if the Alert Me link is displayed within the Search Results:

Team Site - Discussions List - Management

There are no items to **show** in this view of the "Discussions List" list ... To add a new item, click "New

sp2013srv/Lists/Community Discussion/Management.aspx

How To Use This Library

How to use this wiki library You can use this wiki library to share knowledge, brainstorm ideas, collaborate with your team on ... This will **show** you any pages which link to this page ...

sp2013srv/SitePages/How To Use This Library.aspx

Administrator - Style Library

There are no items to **show** in this view of the "Style Library" document library ... To add a new item, click "New" or "Upload

sp2013srv:8080/personal/administrator/.../Forms/AllItems.aspx

5 results

Alert Me   Preferences   Advanced Search

Click OK in the web part properties to save any changes to the Search Results web part:

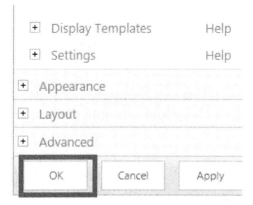

Check in the page:

Publish the page:

⚠ **Recent draft not published** Visitors can't see recent changes. Publish this draft. ⇐

YOU WILL NEED TO MAKE SIMILAR CHANGES TO THE OTHER RESULT PAGES FOR CONSISTENCY.

Allowing Users to Sort Search Results

In previous versions of SharePoint, the out-of-the-box search results provided links to show results by relevance or modified date. Now, with SharePoint 2013, the results may be sorted by any managed property but there are a few preset values. However, by default, the sort option is not enabled.

The Show sort dropdown option allows the user to sort the search results. I personally like this option and the customization of the sort dropdown is covered within the bonus chapters.

The sort options are controlled by the JSON in the Available sort orders text box. You may modify this to add or remove sort options. You may use any managed properties that have been configured in the Search Schema as Sortable.

After checking the Show sort dropdown and saving the web part changes, the sort option displays a dropdown in the search results for sorting purposes:

Adding People to Everything Results

This section demonstrates the use of Promoted Block Results to add People to the Everything Results page.

Once again, the main search results, which is now called Everything, does not include People search results. So it's not really everything. The reason is because there is a special People Search Results web part that is catered towards the User Profiles and their respective properties. If I searched for my last name, my personal profile result does not appear:

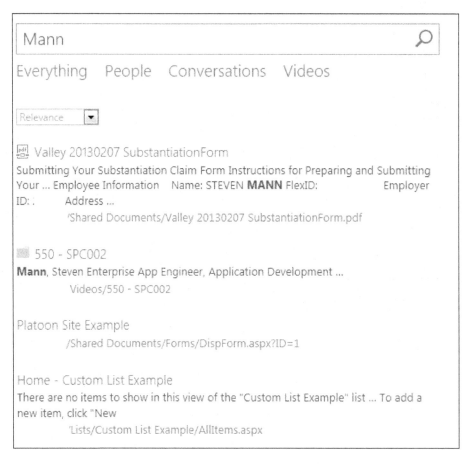

With SharePoint 2013 Search capabilities, you may add people results into your main search (Everything). The rest of this section walks you through the steps.

First go to the site settings of your Search Center and under Site Collection Administration click on Search Query Rules:

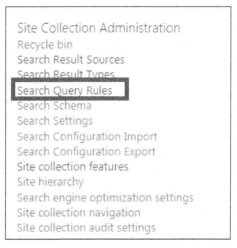

Select Local SharePoint Results (System) in the Context drop-down:

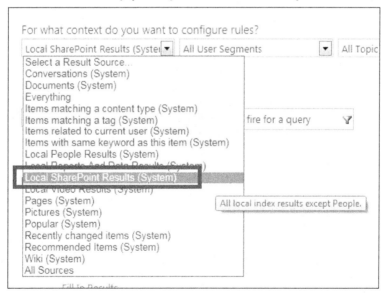

Once that is selected, click on New Query Rule:

On the Add Query Rule page, add a rule name, remove the condition, and then click on the Add Result Block link:

Site Collection Administration › Add Query Rule

(i) **Note:** This query rule will apply to all sites in the site collection. To make one for just this site, use site query rules.

General Information

Rule name

People in Everything

Fires only on source Local SharePoint Results.

▷ Context

Query Conditions

Define when a user's search box query makes this rule fire. You can specify multiple conditions of different types, or remove all conditions to fire for any query text. Every query condition becomes false if the query is not a simple keyword query, such as if it has quotes, property filters, parentheses, or special operators.

Query Matches Keyword Exactly ▾

Query exactly matches one of these phrases (semi-colon separated)

Remove Condition

Add Alternate Condition

Actions

When your rule fires, it can enhance search results in three ways. It can add promoted results above the ranked results. It can also add blocks of additional results. Like normal results, these blocks can be

Promoted Results

Add Promoted Result

Result Blocks
Add Result Block

On the Add Result Block page change the Title to state "People Results". In the Select this Source, select Local People Results (System) and select the amount of items. The default is 2 and that's probably not enough- 3 or 5 seem like good numbers.

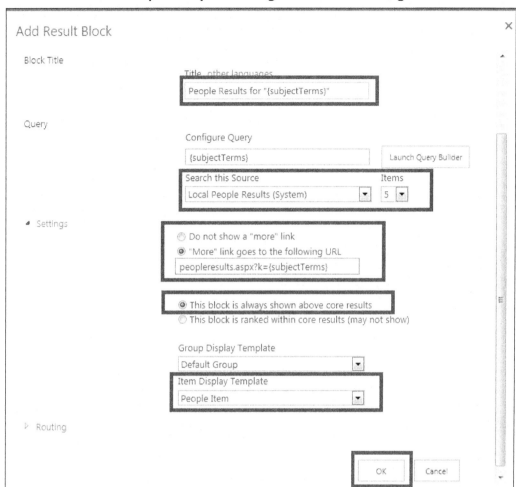

Under the Settings section, as shown above, select the "More" link option and enter "peopleresults.aspx?k={subjectTerms}". Select People Item from the Item Display Template. Click OK.

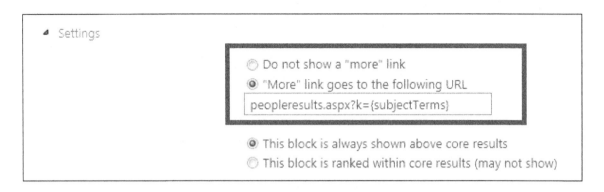

Back on the Add Query Rule page, click Save:

Actions

When your rule fires, it can enhance search results in three ways. It can add promoted results above the ranked results. It can also add blocks of additional results. Like normal results, these blocks can be promoted to always appear above ranked results or ranked so they only appear if highly relevant. Finally, the rule can change ranked results, such as tuning their ordering.

▷ Publishing

Promoted Results

Add Promoted Result

Result Blocks

  Promoted (shown above ranked results in this order)

    Results for "{subjectTerms}" edit remove

Add Result Block

Change ranked results by changing the query

Save   Cancel

Run your search query again (it may take a moment for the changes to appear):

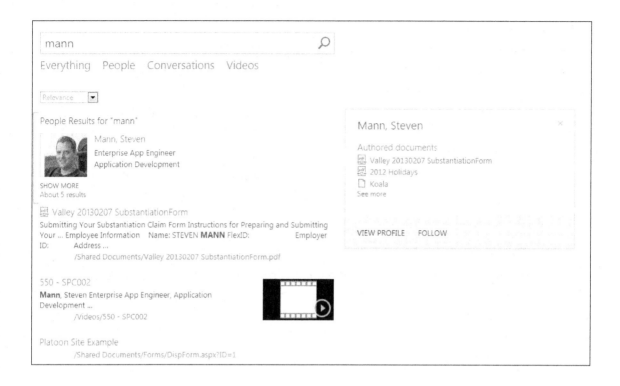

Now you have people results appearing in the search results under Everything!

Adding a Thesaurus for Synonym Results

Synonyms Overview

When people search for items, they may use familiar terms or acronyms accordingly. However, the content may have terms spelled out or contain similar words as the search term but not the same word.

For example, if I search for "Philadelphia" but some content uses "Philly", I won't see those results. Similarly, if I search for "GE" but some content uses "General Electric", I won't see those results either.

This is where synonyms come into play. You may generate and upload a thesaurus file that contains pairs of terms such that when the first term is searched, the second term is also searched.

Create a Thesaurus File

A thesaurus file is a comma separated file which contains three columns: Key, Synonym, and Language. The Language column is optional and therefore your file technically could only contain pairs of synonyms.

An example of thesaurus file contents is as follows:

Key,Synonym,Language

IE,Internet Explorer

Internet Explorer,IE

HR, Human Resources

Human Resources, HR

Notice there is no "vice-versa" implied and therefore for each pair you may want to include the opposite order. Think of it as "when I search for this", "also include this".

To create a thesaurus file, simply open a text editor, add the header, and then go to town adding pairs of synonyms:

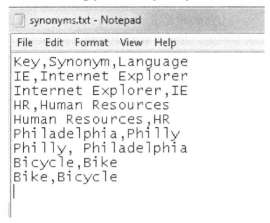

Save the file as a .csv file.

Import a Thesaurus File

In order to import your thesaurus file, you need to use PowerShell.

Launch the SharePoint 2013 Management Console and enter the following two command lines (using your own path for the -FileName parameter):

$ssa= Get-SPEnterpriseSearchServiceApplication

Import-SPEnterpriseSearchThesaurus -SearchApplication $ssa -Filename \\sp2013srv\c$\ThesaurusFile.csv

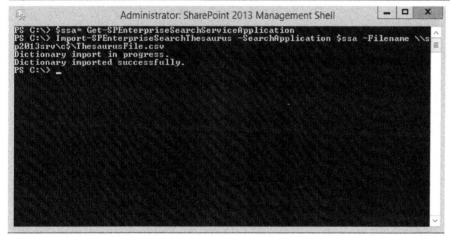

The thesaurus file is imported.

Test Synonyms in Search

To test the thesaurus file, simply search for various synonyms that the file contains. I knew with my example external data, that "Bike" was used often but "Bicycle" was not. I included these synonyms in my thesaurus file. Now when I search for Bicycle, I retrieve results that include Bike:

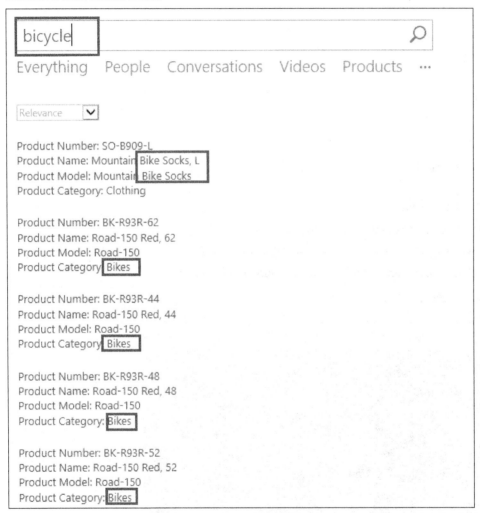

Adding Spelling Words

When looking to summarize the use of spelling words and show examples of the Did You Mean? functionality in SharePoint 2013 Search, I realized that Microsoft MVP, Waldek Mastykarz, already had this topic well summarized on his blog (http://blog.mastykarz.nl). Therefore, with his permission, I have adapted content from his blog post "SharePoint 2013 Query Spelling Inclusions for the masses" to complete this section.

SharePoint 2013 Search provides you with the query spelling suggestion capability that suggest correcting spelling mistakes in search queries. By default this capability is configured to automatically build the spelling suggestions dictionary. By changing the configuration settings it is possible to manually maintain the query spelling suggestions dictionary.

Spelling Words Overview

One of the biggest investments in SharePoint 2013 was the integration of the enterprise-class search engine, previously known as FAST, with the SharePoint Search engine. As a result SharePoint 2013 Search offers us top of the class search capabilities.

Among all the different search-related capabilities of SharePoint 2013 Search are query spelling suggestions – also known as 'did you mean'. Whenever you enter a search query, SharePoint 2013 Search will check if all words have been spelled correctly and if not, it will suggest the correct spelling.

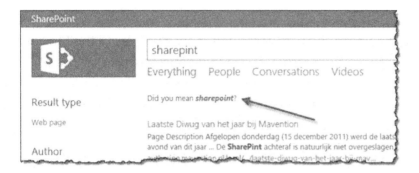

And while the query spelling suggestions do work by default, there are some challenges to how they are configured.

Query Spelling Suggestions

SharePoint 2013 Search knows two types of query spelling suggestion dictionaries: a dynamic and a static one. The dynamic dictionary is maintained by SharePoint itself based on the content in the search index, while the static one is maintained by yourself. Out of the box SharePoint uses the dynamic query spelling suggestions dictionary.

For a term to become a part of the dynamic query spelling dictionary, it has to occur in at least 50 documents. The interesting part is however the content alignment process which is used by the dynamic dictionary and which is enabled by default. This process is triggered when the term that occurs the most in the search index has been found in the preconfigured number of documents (1000 by default; can be changed using PowerShell) and then the dictionary is built.

If you are interested in exploring the default configuration of query spelling suggestions you can use the following PowerShell snippet:

$ssa = Get-SPEnterpriseSearchServiceApplication

Get-SPEnterpriseSearchQuerySpellingCorrection -SearchApplication $ssa

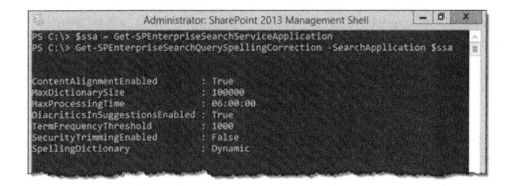

What if, however, you don't want to rely on the standard process of building query spelling suggestions dictionary and want to build and maintain one yourself? The next sub-section explains how to add or remove your own words from SharePoint 2013 Search.

Adding Spelling Words to Your Search Service

Adding spelling words to your search service first involves switching the spelling diction-ary mode to static, and then adding spelling words into the spelling term sets. This sub-section explains both of these processes.

SharePoint 2013 uses two Global Term Sets called **Query Spelling Exclusions** and **Query Spelling Inclusions** to define the query spelling suggestions. Both Term Sets are ignored in the dynamic mode however, so before you can start entering your own suggestions, you have to switch to the static dictionary.

To switch to the static query spelling suggestions dictionary you have to run the follow-ing PowerShell snippet:

$ssa = Get-SPEnterpriseSearchServiceApplication

Set-SPEnterpriseSearchQuerySpellingCorrection -SearchApplication $ssa -SpellingDictionary

This will change the query spelling suggestions dictionary mode to static and with this SharePoint 2013 Search will start using your values stored in the two Term Sets.

Configuring query spelling suggestions is easy and comes down to creating new Terms under the **Query Spelling Exclusions** Term Set (for words which you never want to have suggested) and the **Query Spelling Inclusions** Term Set (for words which SharePoint should suggest). There are a few rules when it comes to configuring query spelling suggestions:

1. a query spelling suggestion is a single word, so **SharePoint** is a correct suggestion but **Sharing Points** is not

2. when creating query spelling suggestions only the first level of Terms is taken into account. SharePoint 2013 Search expects a list of words that it can then use to detect spelling mistakes. Query spelling suggestions Terms are in no way a dictionary such as **SharePint** > **SharePoint**, where the Term **SharePoint** would be a child Term of **SharePint** denoting in a way that every time SharePoint 2013 Search stumbles upon **SharePint** in a search query it should suggest **SharePoint** instead. This part is done by SharePoint automatically without our help.

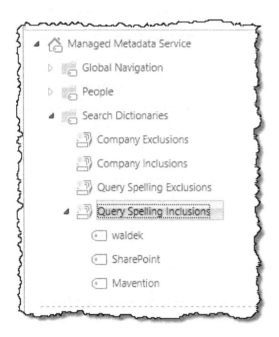

Processing Spelling Words

After you have entered your query spelling suggestions Terms, they won't appear directly in the search results however. Instead you have to wait for the **Search Custom Dictionaries Update** Timer Job to run or execute it manually yourself.

After the job has executed and the query spelling suggestions from the static dictionary have been processed they will be used in SharePoint search results.

Removing Junk Results

Have you ever noticed how much nonsense or irrelevant results come back from various search queries? It's nobody's fault. The content is out there and happens to match the terms we are searching. But do we really need all of this stuff if it's not useful?

I have been recently fine-tuning what comes back in search results. People want content. They don't want containers of content, lists of content, links to content - just plain results they can use. Therefore, I have tweaked my main results to perform the following:

1. Remove excess external content type links and nonsense
2. Remove Folders from search results
3. Remove overall list results (AllItems.aspx)
4. Remove Link List Items
5. Remove Link Lists
6. Remove Explorer Views (web folder results)

I only performed these tweaks on my main results page (a.k.a. Everything) by modifying the query on the Search Results web part:

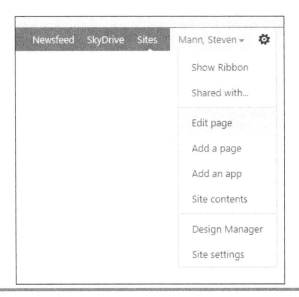

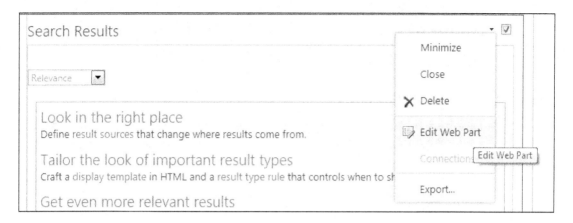

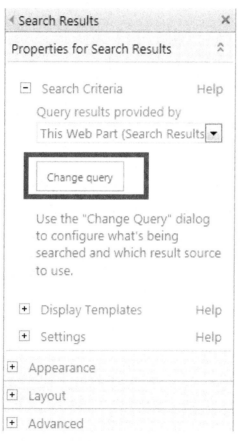

You may perform these tweaks at the Result Source level as well which would probably be the recommended approach. I already had Query Rules associated to the Local SharePoint Results defined by the System.

External Content Type Nonsense

Even though I created custom Result Sources and Result Types for some of my external content data (aka BDC/BCS stuff), I noticed I would still get crazy bdc3:// results back. This was the first thing I removed:

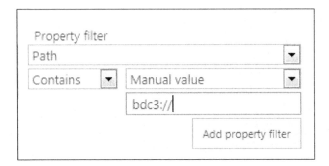

Folders

I noticed folders being returned, which may be correct, but we want content - not the containers of content. I opened one of my folder results and it brought me to a list of --- more folders!! Ahh. We don't need that. Therefore I added another property filter as follows:

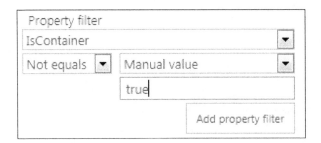

Full List Results (AllItems.aspx)

How many search results show the AllItems.aspx view?? In some queries it's every result. We just need the list item itself, not the full list of irrelevant items. Therefore I decided to filter that out too:

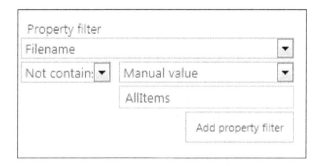

Links List Items

We happen to use many lists of links to display items on various department, office, or home pages. They are convenient and provide an easy way to add a new link to a page. However, for search results, we want links to the main content, not links to links to content. For this I needed to add a filter using the contentclass property:

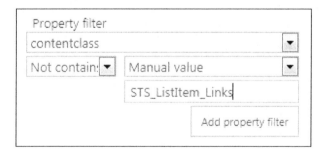

Links Lists

Removing the link items was good but now the entire links list is being returned in results. Might as well remove that too:

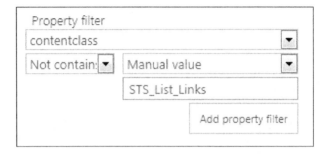

Explorer View

Finally I noticed web folders correlating to Explorer Views of lists being returned. There is no need to gunk up the results with various views. Therefore I filtered these out as well using the secret STS_List_850 contentclass:

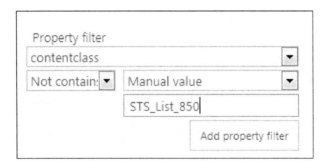

Final Query Text

Here is what I have so far to get all of the junk out of my search results:

Query text

{searchboxquery} -Path:bdc3:// IsContainer<>true -Filename:AllItems -
contentclass:STS_ListItem_Links -contentclass:STS_List_Links -contentclass:STS_List_850

I am now getting cleaner results with mostly documents, posts, relevant list items, cal-
endar items, etc. In addition, I am feeling much better with the improvement on our
relevancy.

Promoting Results

This section demonstrates the promotion of particular results as well as promoted re-sults blocks. The examples here build on top of the Policies result type produced within the end-to-end solution chapters.

Add a Promoted Result to Everything Results

From the end-to-end scenarios discussed in the bonus chapters, I now have a Policies search and results in the navigation. However, if someone searches for a policy in Every-thing, I want to make sure particular results are shown at the top. In this case, when someone searches for "holidays", I want to display the Holiday policy document first. This sub-section explains those steps.

Navigate to your Search Center and select Site Settings from the Settings menu:

Under Site Collection Administration, click on the Search Query Rules link:

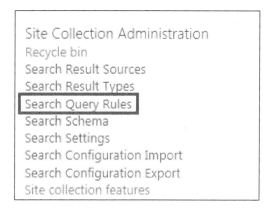

Since I want to promote policy results under Everything, I need to add a query rule to the Local SharePoint Results since that is the result source that is used for Everything.

Select Local SharePoint Results (System) from the Result Source drop-down:

Click on the New Query Rule link:

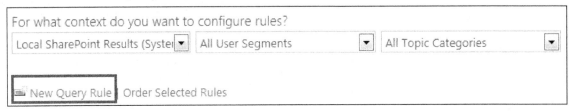

On the Add Query Rule page, enter a Rule name. Add phrases to the text box. Click Add Alternate Condition:

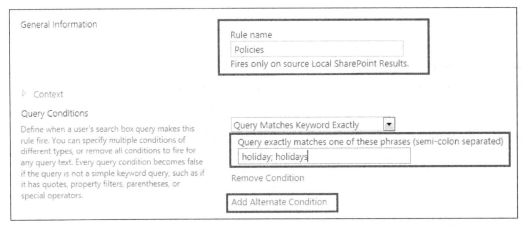

The first query condition matches exactly on the phrases but I want to make sure that this query rule is applied if the search contains any of the phrases as well.

In the second query condition, select Query Contains Action Term and then enter the same phrases into the text box:

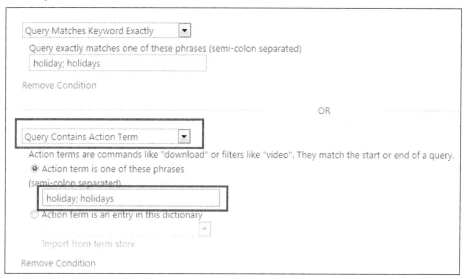

Click on Add Promoted Result:

Actions

When your rule fires, it can enhance search results in three ways. It can add promoted results above the ranked results. It can also add blocks of additional results. Like normal results, these blocks can be promoted to always appear above ranked results or ranked so they only appear if highly relevant. Finally, the rule can change ranked results, such as tuning their ordering.

Promoted Results

Add Promoted Result

Result Blocks
Add Result Block

Change ranked results by changing the query

The Add Promoted Result dialog appears.

Enter a Title and the URL to the document and click Save:

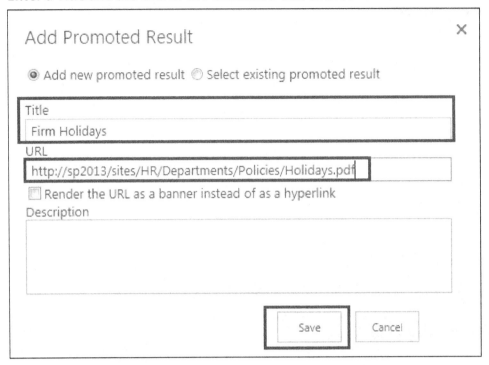

NOTE: The URL can be any internal or external site, document, web page, etc. This example promotes a particular Policy document.

Click Save on the Add Query Rule page.

Test a Promoted Result

Navigate back to your Search center and enter a search term that matches the query rule from the previous section:

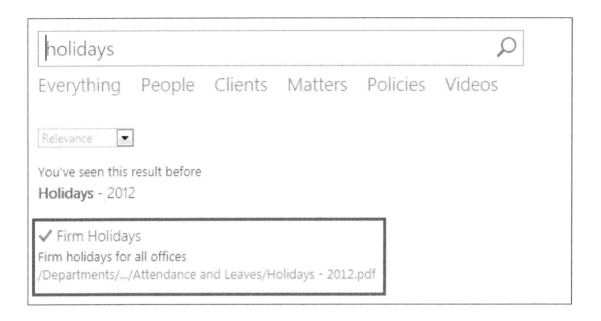

The promoted result is displayed at the top of the results with a blue check mark next to it.

Expand a Promoted Result to Include a Promoted Result Block

From the previous section, I now have a Policies search and results in the navigation. However, if someone searches for a policy in Everything, I want to make sure particular results are shown at the top. In this case, when someone searches for "holidays", I want to display the Holiday policy document first. This section explains those steps.

Navigate to your Search Center and select Site Settings from the Settings menu:

Under Site Collection Administration, click on the Search Query Rules link:

Select Local SharePoint Results (System) from the Result Source drop-down:

Find the query rule created from the previous section and select Edit from the drop-down:

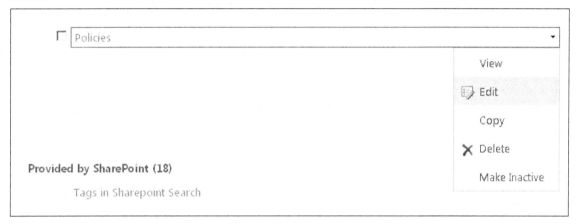

At the bottom of the Query Rule page, click on Add Result Block:

Fill out the Result Block details (similar to adding Everything to People):

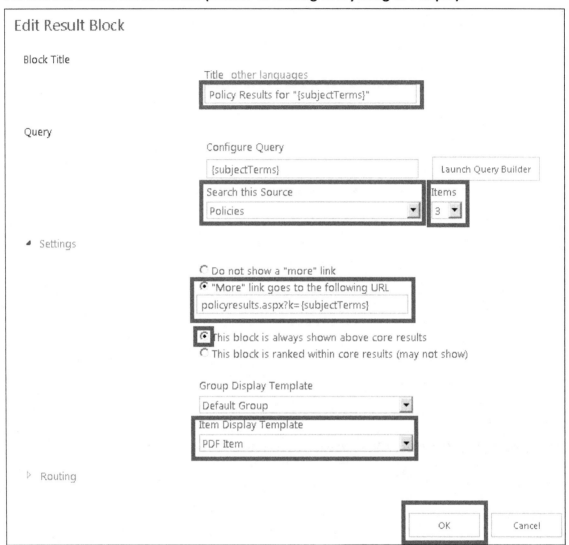

Click OK.

Back on the Query Rule page, click Save. I also expanded my terms and added "office closed" and "offices closed".

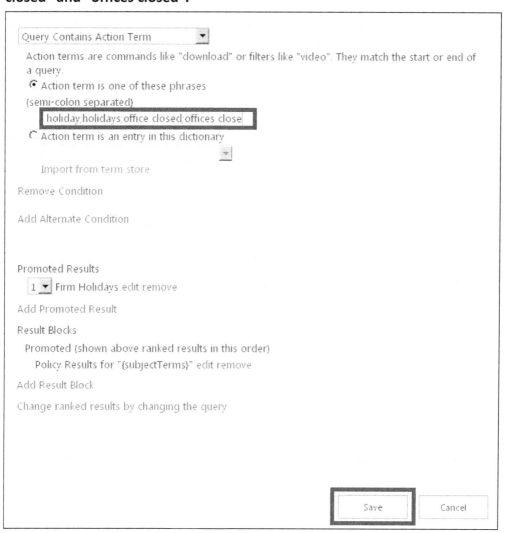

Test Results from a Promoted Result Block

Navigate back to your Search Center and enter terms that match your query rule:

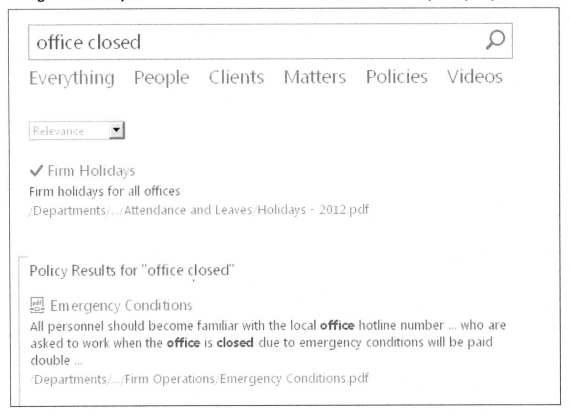

Now both a promoted result and a promoted result block appear when the search terms match the query rule.

Modifying Promoted Result Displays

Promoted Results in SharePoint 2013 take the place of the previous Best Bets. In previous versions of SharePoint, the best bets results used a flashy star. In SharePoint 2013, the icon is no longer a star: it is a blue check mark:

Search uses the Item_BestBet display template to present these promoted results. You may find the template in your Search Display Templates folder:

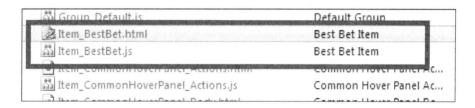

You may make modifications to this template to change how promoted results are rendered. I previously had specific questions at speaking events that dealt with the icon.

There is a div and an img tag located in the template file:

```
<div class="ms-srch-bestBetItem-icon">
    <img id="_#= $htmlEncode(id + Srch.U.Ids.icon) =#_"
</div>
```

This is using a sprite image named searchresultsui.png which is made up of various icons that are used within the search results. Obviously it is using the blue checkmark portion of the sprite. If you wanted, you could modify the image tag to use a different image as the promoted results icon.

```
" src=" #= $urlHtmlEncode(GetThemedImageUrl('searchresultui.png')) =# "
```

Enhancing Search Keywords Using Query Rules

The out-of-the-box query rules provides some instant "keywords" that users may use to force certain types of results to appear. Some rules are setup to look for certain keywords in the beginning of the search phrase or at the end of the search phrase (or both).

For example, the Excel query rule only looks for Excel file extensions in the beginning of the search query but looks for "spreadsheet" and "spreadsheets" (as well as the file extensions without the period) at the end of the search query:

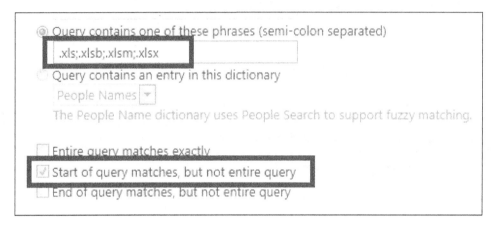

It may be confusing trying to explain to users why results are different based on when and where their keyword appears in their search phrases. It is much easier to say if you use "spreadsheet" in your query, then Excel documents will be returned as a group. Therefore, I have modified all of the out-of-the-box query rules to be consistent in the keywords that are used.

To do this, navigate to your search center

Navigate to your Site Settings from within your Search Center site collection and click on Search Query Rules under Site Collection Administration:

Site Collection Administration
Recycle bin
Search Result Sources
Search Result Types
Search Query Rules
Search Schema
Search Settings
Search Configuration Import
Search Configuration Export
Site collection features
Site hierarchy

Select Local SharePoint Results (System) as the Result Source:

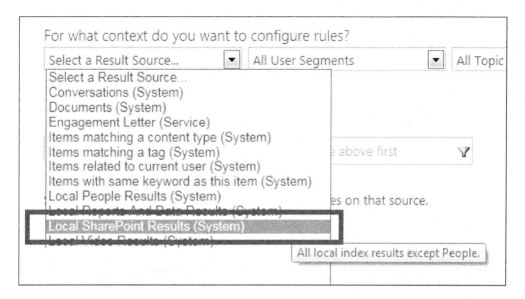

Scroll down to the "Provided By SharePoint" list of query rules. Select the drop-down on one of them and select Copy:

Make sure the rule name has "Copy" in it. This makes it easier to identify that the rule is a customized copy of a query rule provided by SharePoint.

Select the longest list of phrases from the rules:

Notice I also included "excel" as a keyword.

Paste the long list into the other condition:

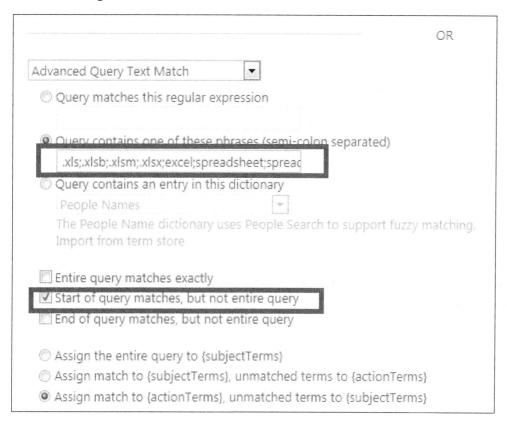

Technically, if you are using the same phrases, the two out-of-the box advanced text match rules may be combined into one where neither the Start nor the End checkboxes are checked.

There is also a third condition from the query rules provided by SharePoint using the Result Type Commonly Clicked option:

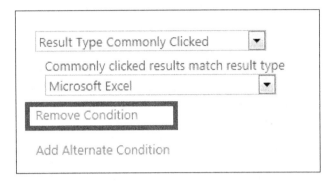

This can be very helpful but also confusing. What this means is if users search for "SharePoint" and always open an Excel document in the results, eventually when others search for "SharePoint" a group of Excel result block will appear in the overall search results. You may or may not want this to occur. **Simply click on the Remove Condition to disable this functionality.**

Scrolling down to the Actions section, you'll see that the query rule, when fired, is set to display the result block within the ranked results:

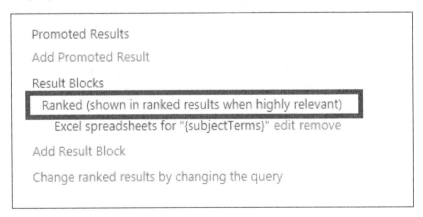

What this means is that the grouping of documents for this rule will appear based on ranking somewhere in the overall results. To the user this may seem like it is just randomly placed. This has the perception of inconsistency.

Therefore, I have modified the result blocks to appear at the top so I can explain to the users that when a "keyword" is used, this forces certain types of document groups to the top of the search results.

To do this, click on the edit link:

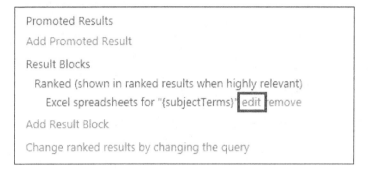

The Edit Result Block dialog appears:

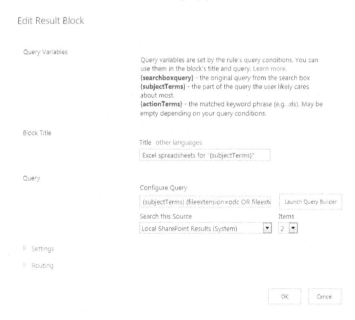

Expand the Settings section and select This block is always shown above core results:

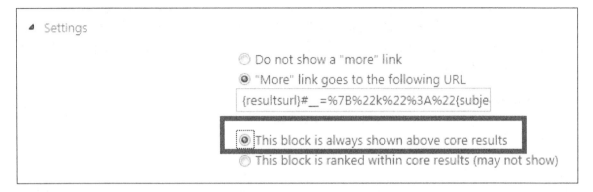

Click OK in the dialog and then click Save on the Query Rule page.

The copied query rule appears under the Defined for this site collection section:

For good measure, I usually scroll back down to the out-of-the-box query rule and make it inactive:

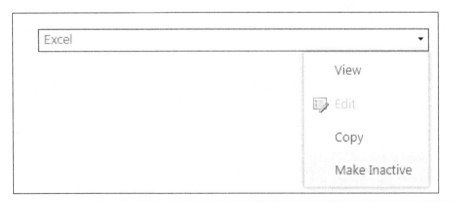

Adding Paging and Counts to the Top

The paging controls along with the number of results are displayed at the bottom of the search results. If you are displaying more than 10 results (or depending on screen resolution), the user has to scroll to the bottom of the results in order to see how many there are or to navigate to the next page of results. However, by customizing the Search Results control display template, you can easily move or add the paging and counts to the top of the results.

Follow the steps outlined in Appendix A to get to the search display templates.

Locate the Control_SearchResults.html file. Right-click and select Edit File in Advanced Mode:

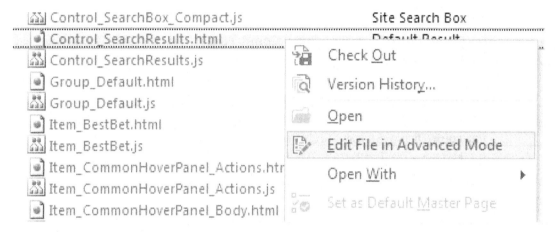

Locate the Paging Code and the Results code at the bottom of the template.

The Paging Code starts with the following:

```
<!--#
            if(ctx.ClientControl.get_showPaging()){
                var pagingInfo = ctx.ClientControl.get_pagingInfo();
                if(!$isEmptyArray(pagingInfo)){
  #-->
```

The Results Code block is as follows:

```
<!--#
            if(ctx.ClientControl.get_showResultCount() &&
ctx.DataProvider.get_totalRows() > 0){
                var start = ctx.DataProvider.get_currentQueryState().s;
                var resultsPerPage = ctx.DataProvider.get_resultsPerPage();
                var totalRows = ctx.DataProvider.get_totalRows();
                var countDisplayString = Srch.Res.rs_ApproximateResultCount;
                if (start + resultsPerPage > totalRows) { countDisplayString = (totalRows ==
1)? Srch.Res.rs_SingleResultCount : Srch.Res.rs_ResultCount; }
  #-->
                                <div class="ms-srch-resultFooter">
                <div id="ResultCount" class="ms-srch-resultscount">
                #= String.format($htmlEncode(countDisplayString), $htmlEn-
code(totalRows.localeFormat("N0"))) =#
                </div>
                </div>
<!--#
                }
  #-->
```

Copy these code blocks and paste them at the top of the display template before the Groups division:

```
184  <!--#_
185            }
186  _#-->
187                    <div id="Groups" class="ms-srch-result-groups">
188  <!--#_
189            ctx.ListDataJSONGroupsKey = "ResultTables";
190  _#-->
191            _#= ctx.RenderGroups(ctx) =#_
192  <!--#_
193            if(ctx.ClientControl.get_shouldShowNoResultMessage()){
194  _#-->
195                    <div id="NoResult" class="ms-srch-result-noResults">
```

Save the changes and run a test search. The paging controls and the result count appear at the top of the results:

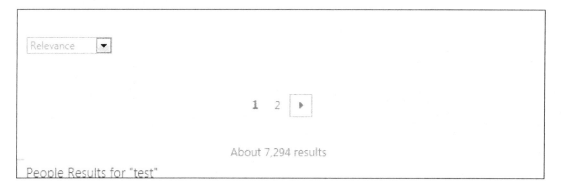

They seem to be spread out a bit and are now taking up some space at the top of the results. You may easily tighten this up a bit by adding the following style property to the Paging <ul>:

<u>style="margin-top:0px;margin-bottom:5px"</u>

```
<!--#_
          if(ctx.ClientControl.get_showPaging()){
              var pagingInfo = ctx.ClientControl.get_pagingInfo();
              if(!$isEmptyArray(pagingInfo)){
#-->
<!--#_
                  <ul id="Paging" class="ms-srch-Paging" style="margin-top:0px;margin-bottom:5px">
<!--#_
                  for (var i = 0; i < pagingInfo.length; i++) {
                      var pl = pagingInfo[i];
                      if(!$isNull(pl)) {
                          var imagesUrl = GetThemedImageUrl('searchresultui.png');
                          if(pl.startItem == -1) {
```

Refresh the search results page to review the modification:

The paging and result count is not so spread out now.

Consistent Search Results (Case)

When I took a class called "Information Retrieval Systems" back in the 90's at Drexel University I never thought I would have to deal with what we learned directly. While the course covered things like stop words (noise words), lingusitics, synonyms, and basic retrieval of information, it really was the foundation for what search engines are built around today.

My professor's classic example was "Time Flies Like an Arrow" and "Fruit Flies Like an Apple". In the first phrase we want "flies" to be a verb but in the second phrase we want "flies" to be a plural noun. Hmmm...to a computer-based search engine they are words that will be searched against a content index and there really is no context around the meanings.

Same problem exists today when users want searches to produce the results they expect versus what the search engine actually finds and deems relevant. The specific problem I solved in SharePoint 2013 Search dealt with searching for "401K".

There are several ways someone may search for 401K -> 401K, 401 K, 401-K, and 401(K). Each of these phrases without any tinkering will produce a different set of results. I found that 401K and 401(K) produced the same number of results essentially because the parenthesis are ignored. So at least I had that covered.

The main problem is "401 K" because of the space. This produces results where there is just a 401 by itself or maybe a K by itself (as a middle initial for example). The "401-K" also produced different results as some content may actually contain the dash.

I originally thought this could all be solved just by using synonyms in my SharePoint 2013 Search thesaurus file (which you upload into Search using PowerShell). That was not the case. Then I thought I could solve the problem with a query rule - also not the case.

It turns out I needed to use a combination of thesaurus entries and a query rule to get the exact same number of results for any 401K combination. The ranking may change based on which version the user enters but as long as they get all of the possible results for each version we are making fruit fly.

Since 401K and 401(K) are treated the same, my thesaurus file contained the following:

Key,Synonym,Language
401 K,401K
401 K,401-K
401K,401 K
401K,401-K
401-K,401K
401-K,401 K

My condition for the query rule was based on if any version of 401K was entered:

Query Conditions

Define when a user's search box query makes this rule fire. You can specify multiple conditions of different types, or remove all conditions to fire for any query text. Every query condition becomes false if the query is not a simple keyword query, such as if it has quotes, property filters, parentheses, or special operators.

Query Matches Keyword Exactly ▾

Query exactly matches one of these phrases (semi-colon separated)

401 k;401(k);401k;401-k

Remove Condition

Add Alternate Condition

The action for the query rules was to change the ranked results by changing the query:

Actions

When your rule fires, it can enhance search results in three ways. It can add promoted results above the ranked results. It can also add blocks of additional results. Like normal results, these blocks can be promoted to always appear above ranked results or ranked so they only appear if highly relevant. Finally, the rule can change ranked results, such as tuning their ordering.

Promoted Results

Add Promoted Result

Result Blocks
Add Result Block

Change ranked results by changing the query
"401(K)" OR "401K" OR "401-K" OR "401 K"
remove changes to query

Essentially I am using quotes to produce exact matches in the content which eliminates any extra results and, by combining with OR statements, I am assuring I get everything out there no matter how 401K is represented.

I really thought the query rule by itself would solve the problem but the synonyms helped seal the deal:

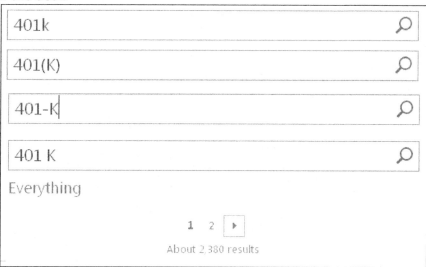

My SharePoint 2013 Search instance is now displaying the same number of results with each version of the search term.

THIS PAGE INTENTIONALLY BLANK

CHAPTER 4

Enhancing Video Results

This chapter walks through the several enhancements that may be achieved with video-based search results.

Implementing a Videos Query Rule

In SharePoint 2013 Search there are several out-of-the-box query rules to display ranked result blocks of various result types (.e.g Word, Excel, PowerPoint, etc.). These are triggered based on specific action terms that appear either in the beginning or end of a search query (or both). However, Videos is not one of them.

Therefore, it would be nice if someone performed a search query using "video" or "videos" that a promoted result block of video results would appear at the top of the results. Easier done than said!

Navigate to your Site Settings from within your Search Center site collection and click on Search Query Rules under Site Collection Administration:

Site Collection Administration
Recycle bin
Search Result Sources
Search Result Types
Search Query Rules
Search Schema
Search Settings
Search Configuration Import
Search Configuration Export
Site collection features
Site hierarchy

Select Local SharePoint Results (System) as the Result Source:

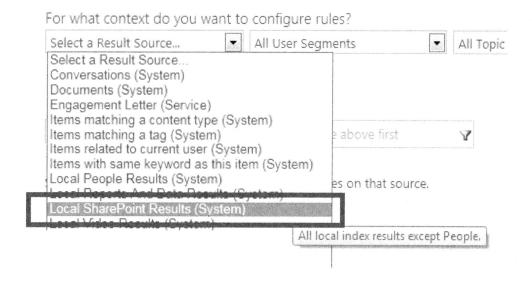

Click on the New Query Rule link:

Add the Rule Name, select Query Contains Action Term, enter "video;videos" in the Action term is one of these phrases:

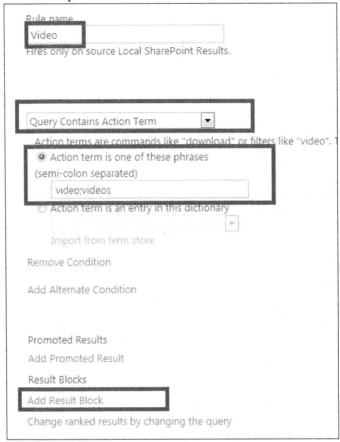

Click on Add Result Block.

Modify the Block Title. Change Search this Source to Local Video Results (System) and increase the amount of Items as desired (I used 6). Expand the Settings section.

Select the "More" link since there is already a Video Results page and enter the value shown in the image below. Select Video Item as the Display Template:

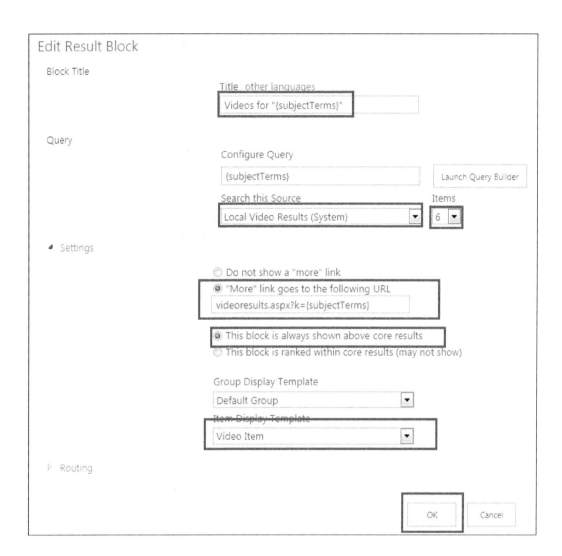

Click OK and then click Save on the New Query Rule page.

Navigate to your Search Center main page and perform a search using "videos" in the query:

Videos for "sharepoint"

SharePoint Youtube

/Video Library/SharePoint Youtube

SharePoint in Plain English

Mann, Steven Enterprise App Engineer, Application Development ...

../Videos/SharePoint in Plain English

SharePoint Video

/sites/Videos/Videos/SharePoint Video

What is **SharePoint**

Mann, Steven Enterprise App Engineer, Application Development ...

/sites/Videos/Videos/What is SharePoint

Top Benefits of **SharePoint** 2013

Mann, Steven Enterprise App Engineer, Application Development ...

/sites/.../Videos/Top Benefits of SharePoint 2013

Tour **SharePoint** 2013 User Interfaces

Mann, Steven Enterprise App Engineer, Application Development ...

/sites/.../Tour SharePoint 2013 User Interfaces

The video result block appears at the top and displays the video results. The results show hover panels when moused over.

Display Video Results Horizontally

There is another way to display these results using an out-of-the-box horizontal video display template. If you go back into your Search Query Rules, edit the Video query, and then edit the Result Block, you may change the Display Template setting to just the Video entry:

Now the results are displayed horizontally along the top:

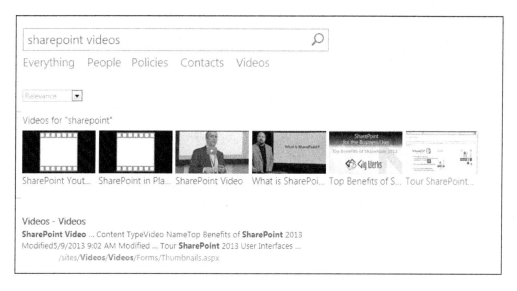

This presents well but there is no hover! You can easily modify the template (or make a new copy as the recommended approach) to display the hover. Those steps are in the next section.

Adding a Hover Panel to the Video Horizontal Display Template

The previous section demonstrated how to display Video results in a horizontal fashion using the out-of-the-box Video horizontal template. However, this display does not incorporate a hover panel and thus nothing pops up when mousing over the results. No problem. You may add a hover panel to the template in just a few easy steps.

First, navigate to the Search Center display templates via SharePoint Designer 2013, similar to the process explained in Appendix A. For simplicity, these steps discuss modifying the display template file in-place but the recommended approach would be to make a copy and use that.

Locate the Item_Video_CompactHorizontal.html file, right-click, and select Edit File in Advanced Mode:

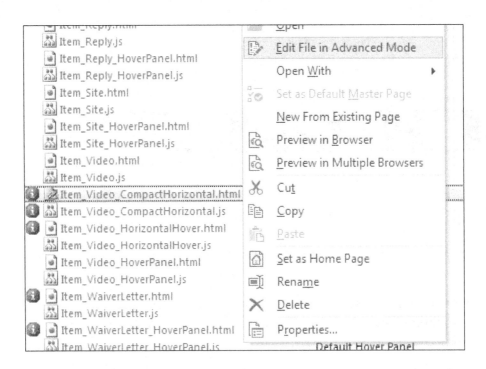

Paste this code at the top as shown in the image below:

```
var id = ctx.ClientControl.get_nextUniqueId();
var itemId = id + Srch.U.Ids.item;
var hoverId = id + Srch.U.Ids.hover;
var hoverUrl = "~sitecollection/_catalogs/masterpage/Display Templates/Search/Item_Video_HoverPanel.js";
$setResultItem(itemId, ctx.CurrentItem);
ctx.currentItem_ShowHoverPanelCallback = Srch.U.getShowHoverPanelCallback(itemId, hoverId, hoverUrl);
ctx.currentItem_HideHoverPanelCallback = Srch.U.getHideHoverPanelCallback();
```

Notice this is using the out-of-the-box Item_Video_HoverPanel .

Next, scroll down to the main <div> and change the id to use _#= $htmlEncode(itemId) =#_

```
mediaDuration.overrideValueRenderer(formatTimeFromSeconds);
_#-->
        <div class="ms-srch-video-intent ms-srch-video-intent-container" id=" _#= $htmlEncode(itemId) =#_ " data-displaytemplate="VideoIntentIt
            <div id="_#= $htmlEncode(hoverId) =#_ " class="ms-srch-hover-outerContainer"></div>
            <div class="ms-srch-video-results-centered ms-srch-video-intent">
                <a clicktype="Result" href="_#= linkUrl =#_" title="_#= $htmlEncode(line1.value) =#_" id="_#= pathId =#_ ">
                    _#= imageMarkup =#_
                </a>
            </div>
            <div class="ms-srch-video-intent-data">
                <h3>
                    <a clicktype="Result" href="_#= linkUrl =#_" title="_#= $htmlEncode(line1.value) =#_" class="ms-srch-video-intent ms-srch-
                        _#= line1 =#_
                    </a>
                </h3>
<!--#_
if ('mediaDuration.isNull)
_#-->
                        _#= mediaDuration =#
```

Add the following code to that very same <div> tag:

onmouseover="_#= ctx.currentItem_ShowHoverPanelCallback =#_ "
onmouseout="_#= ctx.currentItem_HideHoverPanelCallback =#_ "

```
tem" onmouseover="_#= ctx.currentItem_ShowHoverPanelCallback =#_" onmouseout="_#= ctx.currentItem_HideHoverPanelCallback =#_">




h-video-results ms-srch-item-link ms-noWrap" id="_#= line1Id =#_">
```

Now add the following <div> after the first <div>:

<div id="_ #= $htmlEncode(hoverId) =#_ " class="ms-srch-hover-outerContainer"></div>

```
_#-->
<!--#_

        if (!Srch.U.n(ctx.CurrentItem.ParentTableReference) && ctx.CurrentItem.ParentTableReference.TotalRows > 1) {
_#-->

<div id="_ #= $htmlEncode(itemId) =#_ " name="Item" class="ms-srch-people-intentItem" onmouseover="_#= ctx.currentIt
    <div id="_ #= $htmlEncode(hoverId) =#_ " class="ms-srch-hover-outerContainer"></div>
  <div id="VideoCard">
    <ul id="VideoCard">
      <li class="ms-srch-video-itemthumbnail">
        <a clicktype="Result" href="_ #= titleLinkUrl =#_ " id="_ #= thumbnailPathId =#_ ">
          _#= imageMarkup =#_
            <div class="ms-srch-video-playbutton ms-srch-video-playbutton-result"><span></span></div>
        </a>
      </li>
      <li class="ms-srch-video-itemmain">
        <div id="_ #= $htmlEncode(id + Srch.U.Ids.title) =#_ " class="ms-srch-item-title">
          <h3>
            <a clicktype="Result" id="_ #= $htmlEncode(id + Srch.U.Ids.titleLink) =#_ " href="_ #= titleLinkU
              _#= Srch.U.trimTitle(title, maxTitleLengthInChars, termsToUse) =#_
            </a>
          </h3>
        </div>
      </li>
    </ul>
  </div>
</div>
<!--#_
```

Save the changes to the template.

Navigate to your Search Center and perform a search that returns Video results:

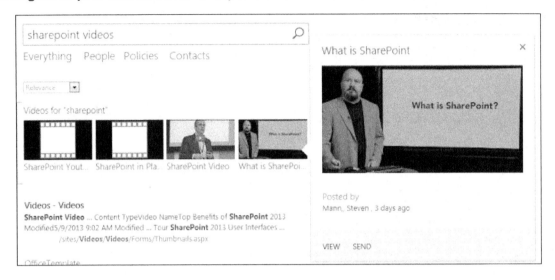

Hovering over the results shows the hover panel preview!!!

CHAPTER 5

Enhancing Image and Picture Results

This chapter walks through the configuration and behaviors of image/picture search results. Without any modifications to your search center and search service application, the crawling and presentation of image/picture items may not always be consistent.

Previewing of Images Not Stored in Picture Libraries

When images are stored in "regular" document libraries such as Site Assets, they are up-loaded as documents. When the library is crawled, the results are the actual list item and not the image itself. Even if you add the Image or Picture content type to the library and modify the item, the result is still treated like a list item. The reason the images are coming back as items is because image file types such as .jpg and .gif are not in the list of the search file types. To correct this, follow the steps in this section.

Launch Central Admin:

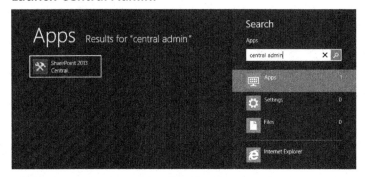

Click on Manage service applications:

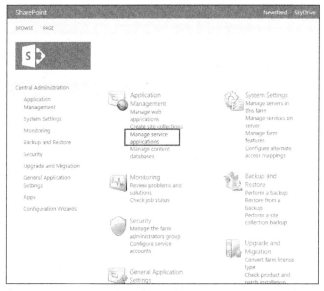

Click on Search Service Application:

On the left hand side click on File Types:

Search Service Application: Manage Content Sources

Use this page to add, edit, or delete content sources, and to manage crawls.

Central Administration

Farm Search Administration

Search Administration

Diagnostics
Crawl Log
Crawl Health Reports
Query Health Reports
Usage Reports

Crawling
Content Sources
Crawl Rules
Server Name Mappings
File Types
Index Reset
Pause/Resume
Crawler Impact Rules

New Content Source | Refresh | ▶ Start all crawls

Type	Name	Status	Current crawl duration	Last crawl duration	Last crawl completed	Next Full Crawl
	Local SharePoint sites	Idle		00:04:00	2/22/2013 1:51:18 PM	None
	Clients	Idle				None

On the File Types page, click on New File Type:

Search Service Application: Manage File Types

Use this page to specify file types to include in the content index.

New File Type

Icon	File name extension
	ascx
	asp
	aspx
	csv
	doc
	docm
	docx
	dot
	dotx
	eml

Enter an image file type such as jpg and click ok:

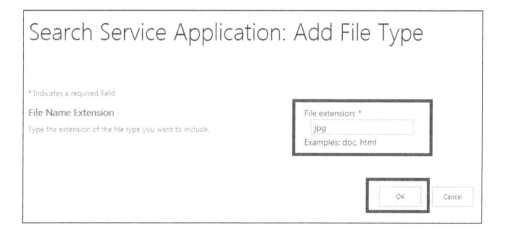

Search Service Application: Add File Type

* Indicates a required field

File Name Extension

Type the extension of the file type you want to include.

File extension: *

jpg

Examples: doc, html

OK   Cancel

Repeat the process for other gif, png, tif, etc. or any other image types you want to handle.

Run a full crawl.

After the crawl is completed, the search results of the images should appear as their filename instead of a list item.

Previewing of Images Stored In Picture Libraries

After going through the steps in the previous section, it turns out even images stored in Picture Libraries are returned as files themselves. The hover works fine but you should be able to take advantage of the image result type. This section corrects that issue.

In your Search Center site collection select Site settings from the settings menu:

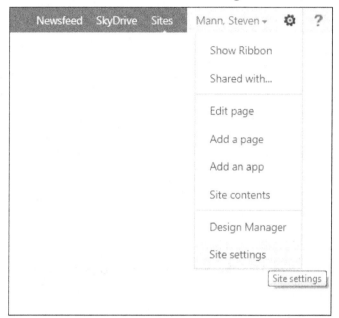

Under Site Collection Administration, click on Search Result Types:

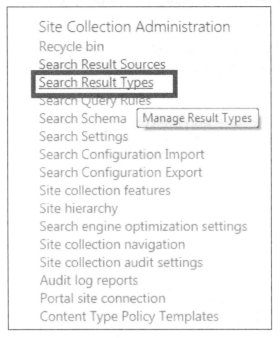

Scroll down and find Image. Use the drop-down menu and select Copy:

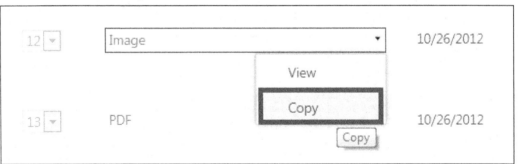

On the Add Result Type page, select Picture Item under What should these results look like?

Site Collection Administration · Add Result Type

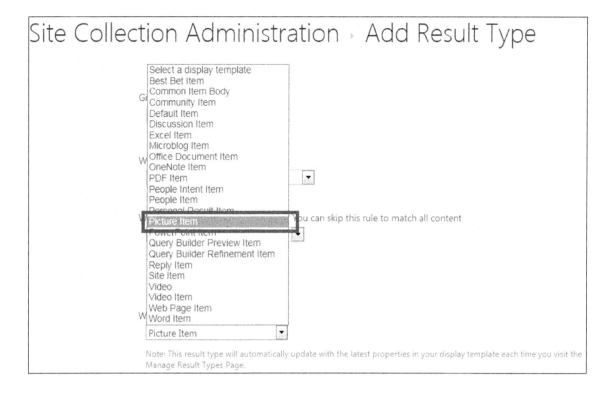

Click Save:

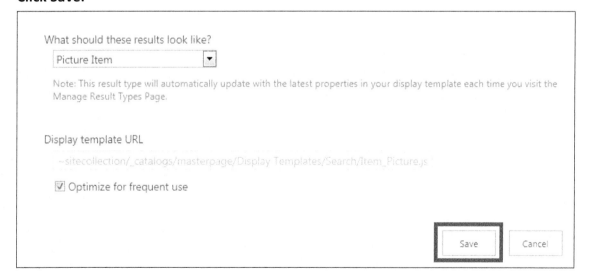

Run a search for an item in a Picture Library:

desert

Everything   People   Conversations   Videos

Desert
Desert.jpg ... Pic Lib/**Desert**.jpg
./Pic Lib/**Desert**.jpg

Home - Pic Lib - All Pictures
Type   Name   Picture Size File Size   Modified ... **Desert**   1024 x 768 827 KB
2/22/2013 1:46 PM ... Lighthouse   1024 x 768 549 KB 2/22/2013 1:45 PM
Pic Lib/Forms/AllItems.aspx

There is a preview image right in the results! That's great but that didn't happen in image results from other types of libraries - on to the next section.

Consistent UX for Images Results

After performing the steps in the previous sections, the results from a Picture Library and non-Picture Library look different. It is not consistent for the user:

You may correct this by editing the Picture Item display template (Item_Picture.html).

(See Appendix A for the main initial steps using SharePoint Designer 2013)

Simply add an else statement to the if in the middle of the code:

```
else {
ctx.CurrentItem.csr_PreviewImage = ctx.CurrentItem.Path;
}
```

```
#-->
        <div id="_#= $htmlEncode(itemId) =#_" name="Item" data-displaytemplate="PictureItem" class="ms-srch-item" onmouseover="_#

]--#_
        if(!Srch.U.n(ctx.CurrentItem.PictureThumbnailURL) && !ctx.CurrentItem.IsContainer) {
            ctx.CurrentItem.csr_PathLength = Srch.U.pathTruncationLengthWithPreview;
            ctx.CurrentItem.csr_PreviewImage = ctx.CurrentItem.PictureThumbnailURL;
        }
        else {
            ctx.CurrentItem.csr_PreviewImage = ctx.CurrentItem.Path;
        }

#-->

        _#=ctx.RenderBody(ctx)=#_
        <div id="_#= $htmlEncode(hoverId) =#_ " class="ms-srch-hover-outerContainer"></div>
    </div>
]--#_
    ]
#-->
    </div>
```

Save the file and run a search again:

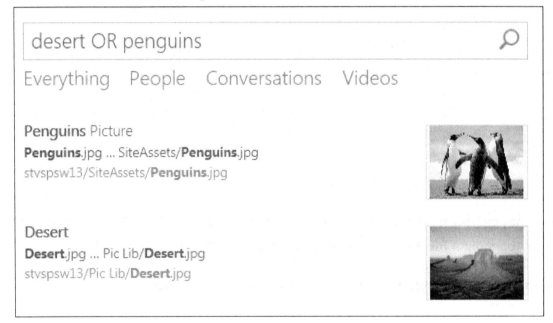

Now all images that are returned have a preview image in the results!!!!

Displaying a Preview Image in the Image Search Result Hover Panel

Hovering over the image search results does not show a larger preview image:

Modify the Item_Picture_HoverPanel.html file and add the following code right before the first if statement:

```
<div class="ms-srch-hover-imageContainer">
<img id=" #= ctx.CurrentItem.csr_id =# " src=" #= $urlHtmlEncode(ctx.CurrentItem.Path) =# " on-
load="this.style.display='block';" />
</div>
```

```
        <div class="ms-srch-hover-innerContainer ms-srch-hover-standardSize" id="_#= $htmlEncode(id + HP.ids.inner) =#_">
            <div class="ms-srch-hover-arrowBorder" id="_#= $htmlEncode(id + HP.ids.arrowBorder) =#_"></div>
            <div class="ms-srch-hover-arrow" id="_#= $htmlEncode(id + HP.ids.arrow) =#_"></div>
            <div class="ms-srch-hover-content" id="_#= $htmlEncode(id + HP.ids.content) =#_" data-displaytemplate="PictureHoverPanel">
                <div id="_#= $htmlEncode(id + HP.ids.header) =#_" class="ms-srch-hover-header">
                    _#= ctx.RenderHeader(ctx) =#_
                </div>
                <div id="_#= $htmlEncode(id + HP.ids.body) =#_" class="ms-srch-hover-body">

                    <div class="ms-srch-hover-imageContainer">
                        <img id="_#= ctx.CurrentItem.csr_id =#_" src="_#= $urlHtmlEncode(ctx.CurrentItem.Path) =#_" onload="this.
                    </div>

! --#_
                if(!Srch.U.n(ctx.CurrentItem.PictureURL)){
                    ctx.CurrentItem.csr_DataShown = true;

                    <div class="ms-srch-hover-imageContainer">
                        <img id="_#= $htmlEncode(id + HP.ids.preview) =#_" alt="_#= $htmlEncode(Srch.Res.hp_Alt_ImagePreview) =#_
#-->
                    </div>
!--#_
                }|
```

Save the file and refresh the search results. A larger image shows in the hover now:

Displaying Image Results Horizontally (with Hover)

SharePoint 2013 contains templates to display both videos and people in a horizontal fashion presenting a nice presentation in the Everything search results. For an example of the Video horizontal display see the previous chapter.

It would be nice to also have this horizontal functionality for images as well as display the hover panel on the items (since the people and video horizontal displays do not incorporate the hover panel out-of-the-box).

Launch SharePoint Designer 2013 and navigate to the search center display templates (similar to the steps outlined in Appendix A).

Locate the Item_Picture.html, right-click and select Copy:

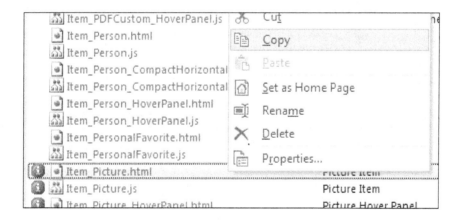

Right-click again and select Paste:

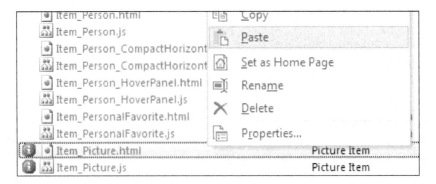

Rename the copied file to Item_Picture_CompactHorizontal:

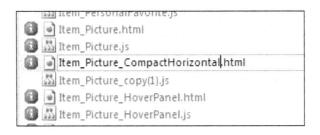

Right-click again and select Edit File in Advanced Mode:

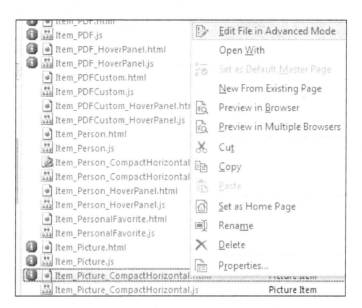

Rename the title and the main div id:

```
<html xmlns:mso="urn:schemas-microsoft-com:office:office" xmlns:msdt="
<head>
<title>Picture Horizontal</title>

<!--[if gte mso 9]><xml>
<mso:CustomDocumentProperties>
<mso:TemplateHidden msdt:dt="string">0</mso:TemplateHidden>
<mso:MasterPageDescription msdt:dt="string">Displays a result tailored
<mso:ContentTypeId msdt:dt="string">0x0101002039C03B61C64EC4A04F5361F38
<mso:TargetControlType msdt:dt="string">;#SearchResults;#</mso:TargetCo
<mso:HtmlDesignAssociated msdt:dt="string">1</mso:HtmlDesignAssociated>
<mso:ManagedPropertyMapping msdt:dt="string">&#39;Title&#39;:&#39;Title
<mso:HtmlDesignStatusAndPreview msdt:dt="string">http://covspwf01/sites
<mso:HtmlDesignConversionSucceeded msdt:dt="string">True</mso:HtmlDesig
</mso:CustomDocumentProperties>
</xml><![endif]-->
</head>
<body>
    <div id="Item_Picture_CompactHorizontal">
<!--#_
        if(!$isNull(ctx.CurrentItem) && !$isNull(ctx.ClientControl)){
            var id = ctx.ClientControl.get_nextUniqueId();
            var itemId = id + Srch.U.Ids.item;
            var hoverId = id + Srch.U.Ids.hover;
```

Add the following code as shown in the image below:

```
<!--#
if (!Srch.U.n(ctx.CurrentItem.ParentTableReference) && ctx.CurrentItem.ParentTableReference.TotalRows > 1)
{
 #-->
```

```
<!--#
} else {
 #-->
```

Scroll to the bottom and add an additional closing bracket:

```
_#-->
                    _#=ctx.RenderBody(ctx)=#_
                    <div id="_#= $htmlEncode(hoverId) =#_"
            </div>
<!--#_
                    [   }   ]
            }
_#-->
        </div>
</body>
</html>
```

Between the if and the else that you pasted first, enter the following code as shown in the image below:

```
<div id="_#= $htmlEncode(itemId) =#_" name="Item" class="ms-srch-people-intentItem" onmouseover="_#=
ctx.currentItem_ShowHoverPanelCallback =#_" onmouseout="_#= ctx.currentItem_HideHoverPanelCallback
=#_">
<div id="ImageInfo">
<!--#_
var pathEncoded = $urlHtmlEncode(ctx.CurrentItem.Path);
var encodedName = $htmlEncode(ctx.CurrentItem.Title);
 _#-->

<ul id="ImageCard">
<li id="ImagePic">
<a clicktype="Result" href="_#= pathEncoded =#_" title="_#= encodedName =#_">
<img id="PicPreview" src="_#= pathEncoded =#_" height="80px" width="80px"/>
</a>
</li>
<li id="ImageTitle">
<div id="imageTitle" class="ms-textSmall ms-srch-ellipsis" title="_#= encodedName =#_">_#= encodedName
=#_</div>
</li>
</ul>
<div id="_#= $htmlEncode(hoverId) =#_" class="ms-srch-hover-outerContainer"></div>
</div>
</div>
```

```
<!--#_
            if (!Srch.U.n(ctx.CurrentItem.ParentTableReference) && ctx.CurrentItem.ParentTableReference.TotalRows
_#-->
      <div id="_#= $htmlEncode(itemId) =#_" name="Item" class="ms-srch-people-intentItem" onmouseover="_#= ctx.
         <div id="ImageInfo">
<!--#_
                  var pathEncoded = $urlHtmlEncode(ctx.CurrentItem.Path);
                  var encodedName = $htmlEncode(ctx.CurrentItem.Title);
_#-->

         <ul id="ImageCard">
            <li id="ImagePic">
               <a clicktype="Result" href="_#= pathEncoded =#_" title="_#= encodedName =#_">
                  <img id="PicPreview" src="_#= pathEncoded =#_" height="80px" width="80px"/>
               </a>
            </li>
            <li id="ImageTitle">
               <div id="imageTitle" class="ms-textSmall ms-srch-ellipsis" title="_#= encodedName =#_">
            </li>
         </ul>
            <div id="_#= $htmlEncode(hoverId) =#_" class="ms-srch-hover-outerContainer"></div>
         </div>
      </div>
<!--#_
            } else {
_#-->
```

Save the changes and then navigate to your Search Center.

From your Search Center site settings, select Search Query Rules from the Site Collection Administration section:

Site Collection Administration
Recycle bin
Search Result Sources
Search Result Types
Search Query Rules
Search Schema
Search Settings
Search Configuration Import
Search Configuration Export
Site collection features

Select the Local SharePoint Results (System):

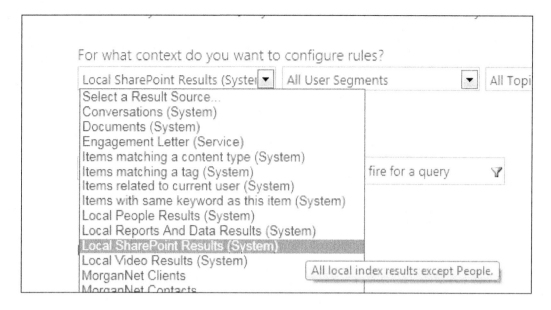

After the Query Rules load on the page, scroll down and find the Image entry. From the drop-down menu select Copy:

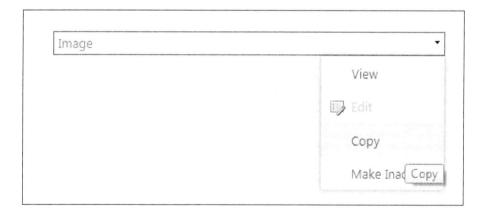

Change the Rule name:

Rule name

Image - Copy

Fires only on source Local SharePoint Results.

Advanced Query Text Match

○ Query matches this regular expression

◉ Query contains one of these phrases (semi-colon separated)

.gif;.jpg;.png;gif;image;images;jpg;photo;ph

○ Query contains an entry in this dictionary

People Names

The People Name dictionary uses People Search to support fuzzy matching.
Import from term store

Scroll down to the Actions sections and click on edit to edit the result block:

Actions

When your rule fires, it can enhance search results in three ways. It can add promoted results above the ranked results. It can also add blocks of additional results. Like normal results, these blocks can be promoted to always appear above ranked results or ranked so they only appear if highly relevant. Finally, the rule can change ranked results, such as tuning their ordering.

Promoted Results

Add Promoted Result

Result Blocks

Promoted (shown above ranked results in this order)

Images for "{subjectTerms}" edit remove

Add Result Block

Change ranked results by changing the query

Change the Query. (I was not getting expected results from the InternalFileType property. Therefore I changed my query filter to "(ContentType:PictureItem OR ContentType:Image)").

I also changed the amount of items to 6:

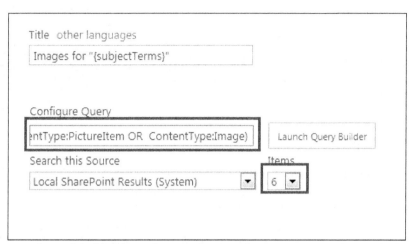

In the Settings select This block is always shown above core results and also change the Item Display Template to the new Picture Horizontal template:

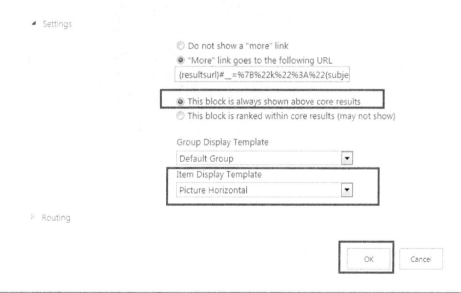

Click OK. Click Save on the Edit Query Rule page.

Navigate to your search page and peform a search for images:

Images for "computer"

04-05-07_1016.jpg   04-05-07_1017.jpg   04-05-07_1018.jpg   04-05-07_1423.jpg   04-05-07_1424.jpg   04-05-07_1425.jpg

SHOW MORE
About 408 results

The images display horizontally and the hover works as well:

computer image

Everything   People

Relevance ▼

Images for "computer"

04-05-07_1016.jpg   04-05-07_1017.jpg

SHOW MORE
About 408 results

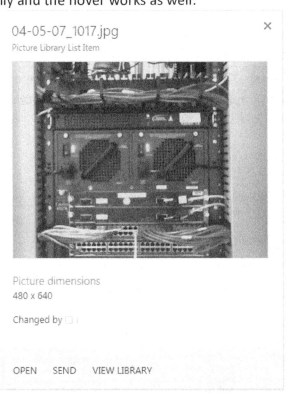

04-05-07_1017.jpg   ×

Picture Library List Item

Picture dimensions
480 x 640

Changed by ☐

OPEN   SEND   VIEW LIBRARY

THIS PAGE INTENTIONALLY BLANK

CHAPTER 6

Enhancing PDF Document Results

This chapter walks through the configuration and behaviors of image/picture search results. Without any modifications to your search center and search service application, the crawling and presentation of image/picture items may not be consistent.

PDF Handling Overview

SharePoint 2013 supports PDF documents out-of-the-box. Initially, web applications do not allow opening PDFs in the browser, however, by adding PDF as an allowed MIME type, browser rendering via Adobe is achieved.

Office Web Apps server provides Office document previews and rendering in Search results without the need for client applications installed (e.g. Word, Excel, etc.). However, once SharePoint is bound to Office Web Apps, PDF documents no longer open in the browser.

There are two workarounds –

1) Configure PDF items to render as Word Items which allows PDFs to open and preview in Search within Office Web Apps
2) Modify the PDF Item display template which allows PDFs to render in the browser via Adobe. Modify the PDF hover template to display previews.

These workarounds take care of Search, but PDFs will still open in the client application (e.g. Adobe) from Document Libraries. The solution here is an update to Office Web Apps. The February/March 2013 Update to Office Web Apps server supports opening PDFs from document libraries within Office Web Apps.

The following table summarizes the various PDF rendering and preview behaviors:

	Search PDF Preview	Search Open (clicking on result)	Document Library Open (clicking on Document)
Out of the Box (Strict Web App)	Available by modifying the Display Template	Opens in Adobe or associated client application	Opens in Adobe or associated client application
Out of the Box (Permissive Web App or Allowed Mime Type of PDF)	Available by modifying the Display Template	Opens in web browser and search term is passed into Adobe	Web Browser
Office Web Apps Server (October 2012 Release)	Two options: 1. Display template (shows in Adobe web) 2. Modify Result Type to use Word Item (shows in Word App Web)	Opens in Adobe or associated client application. Opens in Browser with modification of display template	Opens in Adobe or associated client application.
Office Web Apps Server (Feb/Mar 2013 Update)	Two options: 1. Display template (shows in Adobe web) 2. Modify Result Type to use Word Item (shows in Word App Web)	Opens in browser using Word Web App Can use templates to display in Adobe Web.	Opens in browser using Word Web App If not bound to WordPDF – Opens in Adobe or associated client application.

It is also worth mentioning that if Office Web Apps is not used for Search results of PDFs, the opening of PDFs in the browser passes the search terms into Adobe and thus finds the occurrences within the document. An example of this "search term pass-through" is displayed below:

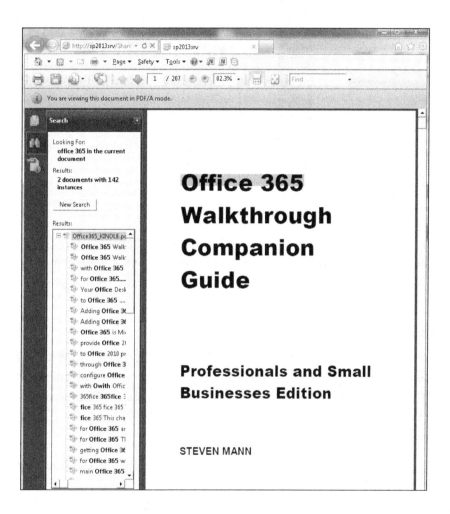

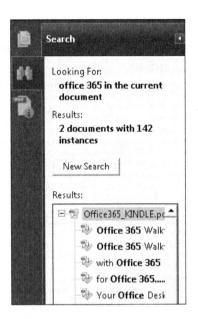

Based on my investigations and modifications, when using Office Web Apps server with SharePoint, there are two overall options when handling PDFs. One provides a more consistent user experience and the other provides the most functionality.

Most Consistent User Experience

The most consistent user experience would be to use Office Web Apps server (with the update) to enable opening of PDFs from libraries in the browser and to modify the search result type to render PDFs as Word Items which enables both preview and opening of the documents from Search results within Office Web Apps.

Most Functionality

The option that provides the most functionality is to use Office Web Apps for document libraries such that PDFs are opened within the browser but then use customized search templates to preview and open PDFs from Search results thus providing the search term pass-through functionality as described above. For the most consistent preview, use a customized copy of the Word item hover panel template.

The rest of this chapter steps through the details and explains how to accomplish the various options and behaviors.

PDF Handling Out-Of-The-Box (without Office Web Apps Server)

Web Applications are created with the Browser File Handling option set to Strict. This means that only the default allowed MIME types (correlates to document types such Word, PDF, etc.) can open and display within the browser without prompting the user to Open or Save the document. PDF is not one of those default MIME types and thus, the user is prompted when attempting to open a PDF document:

The recommended way to enable PDFs to be opened in the browser is to add the MIME type to the allowed list of types by using PowerShell commands:

```
$webApplication = Get-SPWebApplication "http:/yourwebapplicationurl"
$webAppApplication.AllowedInlineDownloadedMimeTypes.Add("application/pdf")
$webApplication.Update()
```

Source: http://social.technet.microsoft.com/wiki/contents/articles/8073.sharepoint-2010-and-2013-browser-file-handling-deep-dive.aspx#DownloadFunctions

The other easy option, which is not recommended, is to modify your web application (via Central Admin) and change the Browser File Handling property to Permissive:

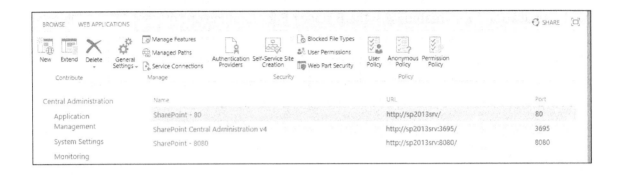

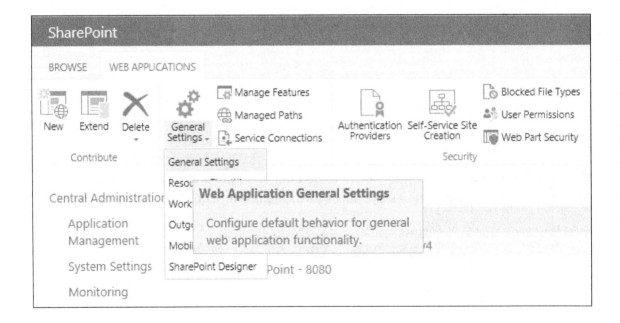

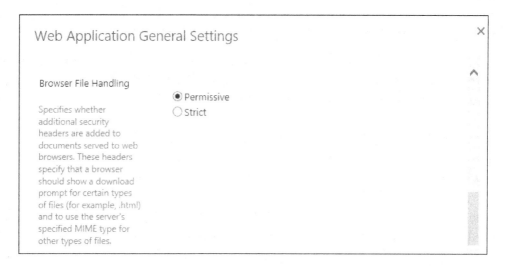

Either method will allow PDF files to be opened in the browser. A neat experience in search results is that the search term is passed into Adobe and the terms are highlighted in the document:

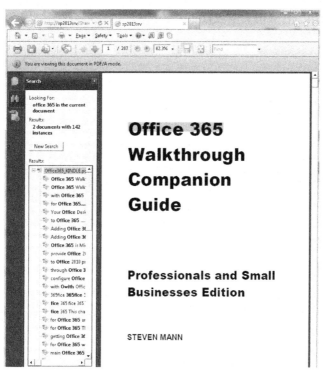

PDF Handling with Office Web Apps October 2012 Release Version

Once Office Web Apps is installed and configured, by surprise, PDF documents no longer open in the browser. Neither from document libraries nor from the search results. So there two options at this point (at least for the search results).

1. Copy the PDF Result Type and use the Word Item template for PDFs. This method both shows a preview and opens up PDF search results in the Office Web App's Word App Viewer. (See section in this chapter for steps).

2. Use my original method for creating a PDF Preview to generate the preview by modifying the Display Templates. (See section in this chapter for the steps).

Follow these steps to allow opening of the PDF document in the browser via Adobe (maintaining the search term pass-through functionality:

Modify the Item_PDF.html in the display templates folder.

Replace this line:

ctx.CurrentItem.csr_OpenControl = "PdfFile.OpenDocuments";

With this one:

ctx.CurrentItem.csr_OpenApp = "word";

```
if(!Srch.U.e(k)){
    ctx.CurrentItem.csr_Path = ctx.CurrentItem.Path + "#search=" + $urlKeyValueEncode(k);
}
ctx.CurrentItem.csr_Icon = Srch.U.getIconUrlByFileExtension(ctx.CurrentItem);
ctx.CurrentItem.csr_OpenControl = "PdfFile.OpenDocuments";
ctx.currentItem_ShowHoverPanelCallback = Srch.U.getShowHoverPanelCallback(itemId, hoverId, hoverUrl);
ctx.currentItem_HideHoverPanelCallback = Srch.U.getHideHoverPanelCallback();
```

```
if(!Srch.U.e(k)){
    ctx.CurrentItem.csr_Path = ctx.CurrentItem.Path + "#search=" + $urlKeyValueEncode(k);
}
ctx.CurrentItem.csr_Icon = Srch.U.getIconUrlByFileExtension(ctx.CurrentItem);
ctx.CurrentItem.csr_OpenApp = "word";
ctx.currentItem_ShowHoverPanelCallback = Srch.U.getShowHoverPanelCallback(itemId, hoverId, hoverUrl);
ctx.currentItem_HideHoverPanelCallback = Srch.U.getHideHoverPanelCallback();
```

Problems solved, right? At this point the search is fixed but PDFs don't open from document libraries in the browser. That's where the Office Web Apps Update comes in to play!

PDF Handling with Office Web Apps Server Public Update (March 2013) using a Hybrid Approach

There was a cumulative and public update released in early March 2013 that adds additional support for PDFs in SharePoint 2013 using Office Web Apps server. The update adds a new application type named WordPDF. It allows PDFs to be opened from document libraries in the browser using the Word App Viewer.

What about search? For search, there is no change. You either need to copy the PDF Result Type and configure it to use the Word Item or modify the search display templates. (Same options as above).

However, I have come up with a hybrid approach that provides a consistent preview using the Word App Viewer but also provides the rendering of PDFs in the browser through Adobe with the search term pass-through!

Open SharePoint Designer and navigate to the search display templates (see Appendix A for these steps).

Find Item_PDF.html. Right-click and select Copy:

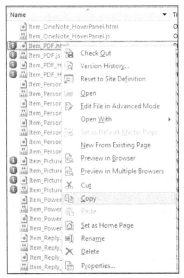

Right-click again and select Paste:

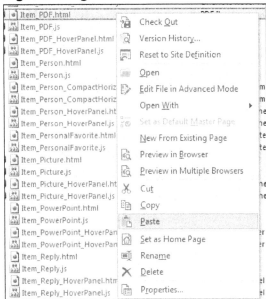

This process creates a copy of the file which appears at the bottom of the list. Find the copy and rename to something different (such as Item_PDFCustom.html):

Right-click the new file and select Edit File in Advanced Mode:

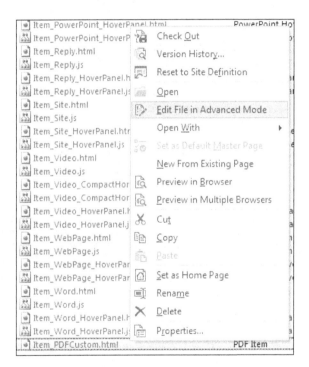

Rename the title:

```
<html xmlns:mso="urn:schemas-microsoft-com:office:offi
<head>
<title>PDF Customized Item</title>

<!--[if gte mso 9]><xml>
<mso:CustomDocumentProperties>
<mso:TemplateHidden msdt:dt="string">0</mso:TemplateHi
<mso:MasterPageDescription msdt:dt="string">Displays a
<mso:ContentTypeId msdt:dt="string">0x0101002039C03B61
<mso:TargetControlType msdt:dt="string">;#SearchResult
<mso:HtmlDesignAssociated msdt:dt="string">1</mso:Html
<mso:ManagedPropertyMapping msdt:dt="string">&#39;Titl
<mso:HtmlDesignConversionSucceeded msdt:dt="string">Tr
<mso:HtmlDesignStatusAndPreview msdt:dt="string">http:
</mso:CustomDocumentProperties>
</xml><![endif]-->
</head>
```

Change the hoverURL:

```
<body>
    <div id="Item_PDF">
<!--#_
    if(!$isNull(ctx.CurrentItem) && !$isNull(ctx.ClientControl)){
        var id = ctx.ClientControl.get_nextUniqueId();
        var itemId = id + Srch.U.Ids.item;
        var hoverId = id + Srch.U.Ids.hover;
        var hoverUrl = "~sitecollection/_catalogs/masterpage/Display Templates/Search/Item_PDFCustom_HoverPanel.js";
        $setResultItem(itemId, ctx.CurrentItem);
        var k = ctx.DataProvider.get_currentQueryState().k;
        if(!Srch.U.e(k)){
            ctx.CurrentItem.csr_Path = ctx.CurrentItem.Path + "#search=" + $urlKeyValueEncode(k);
        }
        ctx.CurrentItem.csr_Icon = Srch.U.getIconUrlByFileExtension(ctx.CurrentItem);
        ctx.CurrentItem.csr_OpenApp = "word";
        ctx.CurrentItem_ShowHoverPanelCallback = Srch.U.getShowHoverPanelCallback(itemId, hoverId, hoverUrl);
        ctx.currentItem_HideHoverPanelCallback = Srch.U.getHideHoverPanelCallback();
```

Replace this line:
ctx.CurrentItem.csr_OpenControl = "PdfFile.OpenDocuments";

With this one:
ctx.CurrentItem.csr_OpenApp = "word";

```
if(!Srch.U.e(k)){
    ctx.CurrentItem.csr_Path = ctx.CurrentItem.Path + "#search=" + $urlKeyValueEncode(k);
}
ctx.CurrentItem.csr_Icon = Srch.U.getIconUrlByFileExtension(ctx.CurrentItem);
ctx.CurrentItem.csr_OpenControl = "PdfFile.OpenDocuments";
ctx.currentItem_ShowHoverPanelCallback = Srch.U.getShowHoverPanelCallback(itemId, hoverId, hoverUrl);
ctx.currentItem_HideHoverPanelCallback = Srch.U.getHideHoverPanelCallback();
```

```
if(!Srch.U.e(k)){
    ctx.CurrentItem.csr_Path = ctx.CurrentItem.Path + "#search=" + $urlKeyValueEncode(k);
}
ctx.CurrentItem.csr_Icon = Srch.U.getIconUrlByFileExtension(ctx.CurrentItem);
ctx.CurrentItem.csr_OpenApp = "word";
ctx.currentItem_ShowHoverPanelCallback = Srch.U.getShowHoverPanelCallback(itemId, hoverId, hoverUrl);
ctx.currentItem_HideHoverPanelCallback = Srch.U.getHideHoverPanelCallback();
```

Save the file.

This handles the opening of the PDF document in the browser. Now for the preview.

Locate Item_Word_HoverPanel.html. Right-click and select copy:

Right-click and select Paste:

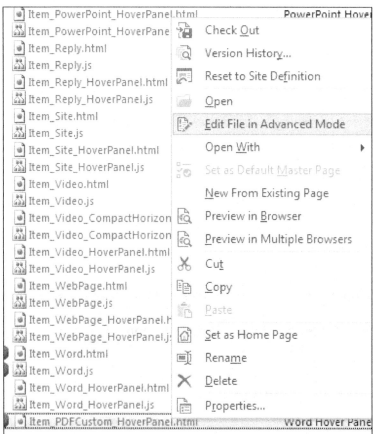

Rename the copied file (should be the same name you used for the hoverUrl value):

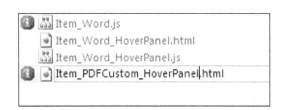

Right-click the new file and select Edit File in Advanced Mode:

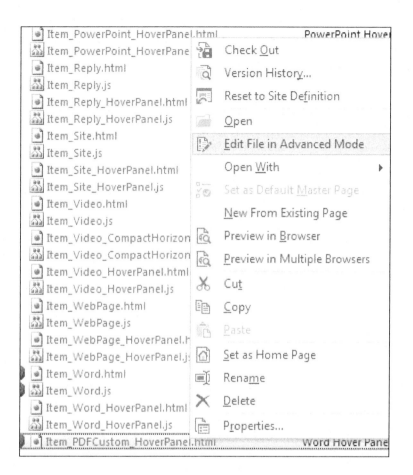

Change the title:

```
<html xmlns:mso="urn:schemas-microsoft-com:office:office" xm
<head>
<title>PDF Custom Hover Panel</title>

<!--[if gte mso 9]><xml>
<mso:CustomDocumentProperties>
<mso:TemplateHidden msdt:dt="string">0</mso:TemplateHidden>
<mso:MasterPageDescription msdt:dt="string">Displays a resul
<mso:ContentTypeId msdt:dt="string">0x0101002039C03B61C64EC4
<mso:TargetControlType msdt:dt="string">;#SearchHoverPanel;#
<mso:HtmlDesignAssociated msdt:dt="string">1</mso:HtmlDesign
<mso:ManagedPropertyMapping msdt:dt="string">&#39;Title&#39;
<mso:HtmlDesignConversionSucceeded msdt:dt="string">True</ms
<mso:HtmlDesignStatusAndPreview msdt:dt="string">http://covs
</mso:CustomDocumentProperties>
</xml><![endif]-->
</head>
<body>
```

Save the Changes.

In your Search Center, select Site Settings from the Settings menu (gear).
Under Site Collection Administration, click on Search Result Types:

Site Collection Administration
Recycle bin
Search Result Sources
Search Result Types
Search Query Rules
Search Schema
Search Settings
Search Configuration Import
Search Configuration Export
Site collection features

Scroll down and find the PDF entry. Select Copy from the drop-down menu:

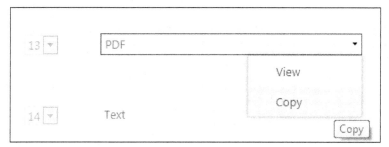

Give the type a unique name and select the PDF Customized Item as the display template:

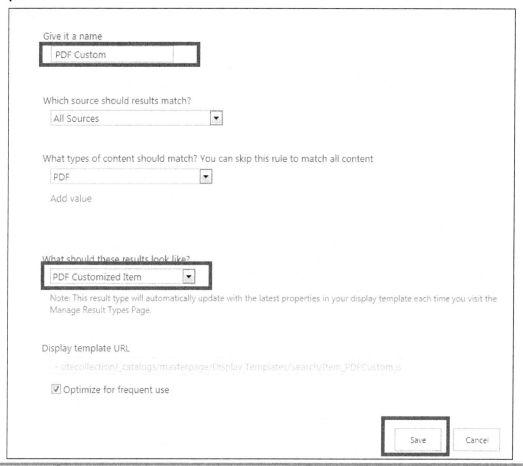

Click Save.

Now, the search results display previews using Office Web Apps:

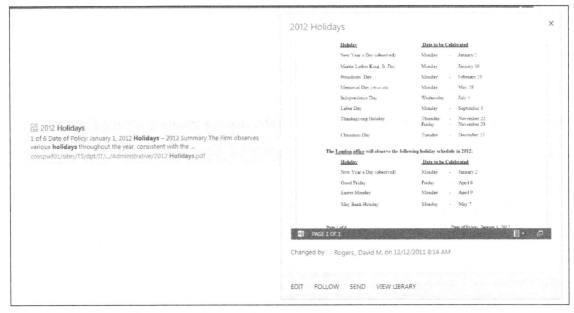

And the documents open in Adobe with the search term pass-through:

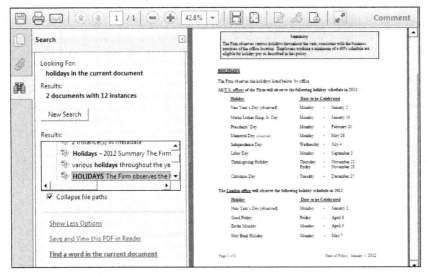

PDF Preview by Modifying Display Templates

This method of PDF previews involves the modification of search display templates. I found it better to modify the templates using SharePoint Designer 2013 although they are accessible through the SharePoint master page UI.

Navigate to the Search Display Templates using SharePoint Designer 2013 as explained in Appendix A.

Right-click on Item_PDF_HoverPanel.html and select Edit File in Advanced Mode

Paste the following code within the most inner <div>

```
<object data="  #= ctx.CurrentItem.Path =#  " type="application/pdf" width="100%"
height="500px" >
<p>It appears you don't have a PDF plugin for this browser/device.
You can <a href="  #= ctx.CurrentItem.Path =#  ">click here to
download the PDF file.</a></p>
</object>
```

```
<div id="Item PDF HoverPanel">
<!--#_
    var i = 0;
    var id = ctx.CurrentItem.csr_id;
    ctx.CurrentItem.csr_ShowFollowLink = true;
    ctx.CurrentItem.csr_ShowLastModifiedTime = true;
    ctx.CurrentItem.csr_ShowAuthors = true;
    ctx.CurrentItem.csr_ShowViewLibrary = true;
_#-->
    <div class="ms-srch-hover-innerContainer ms-srch-hover-standardsize" id="_#= $htmlEncode(id + HP.ids.inner) =#_">
        <div class="ms-srch-hover-arrowBorder" id="_#= $htmlEncode(id + HP.ids.arrowBorder) =#_"></div>
        <div class="ms-srch-hover-arrow" id="_#= $htmlEncode(id + HP.ids.arrow) =#_"></div>
        <div class="ms-srch-hover-content" id="_#= $htmlEncode(id + HP.ids.content) =#_" data-displaytemplate="PDFHoverPanel">
            <object data="  #= ctx.CurrentItem.Path =#  " type="application/pdf" width="500px" height="630px" >
                <p>It appears you don't have a PDF plugin for this browser/device.
                You can <a href="  #= ctx.CurrentItem.Path =#  ">click here to
                download the PDF file.</a></p>
            </object>
            <div id="_#= $htmlEncode(id + HP.ids.actions) =#_" class="ms-srch-hover-actions">
                _#= ctx.RenderFooter(ctx) =#_
            </div>
        </div>
    </div>
</div>
</body>
</html>
```

I actually replaced the Render Header and Render Body divs with the object code.

Save the file.

When saving the file, you may get a warning about breaking from the site definition. Click OK. What happens behind the scenes is that the HTML changes are incorporated into the javascript version of the template (Item_PDF_HoverPanel.js).

Test the results. Perform a search from your search center that produces PDF document results. Hover over the PDF document to see the preview:

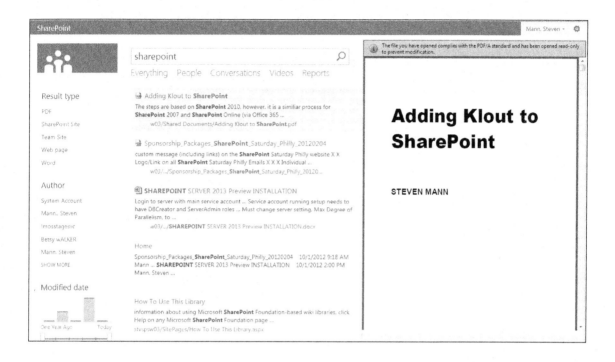

PDF Preview by Copying the Result Type (using Office Web Apps Server)

When using Office Web Apps Server with SharePoint 2013, there is an easier way to present PDF previews without having to modify the search display templates. This involves copying and modifying the PDF result type and have it render as a Word Item.

The first step is to navigate to your Search Center site settings:

Under Site Collection Administration, click on Search Result Types:

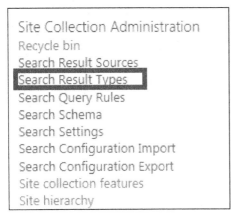

Scroll down and find the PDF entry under the Provided by the search service section. Select Copy from the drop-down menu:

On the Add Result Type page, rename the item and select Word Item under What should these results look like:

Click Save.

Run a full crawl and then perform a search that produces PDF entries. The hover pre-view now uses the Word App Viewer via Office Web Apps Server:

CHAPTER 7

Enhancing the Refinement UX

Modifying the Refinement Web Part

Navigate to a results page and use the Settings menu to edit the page:

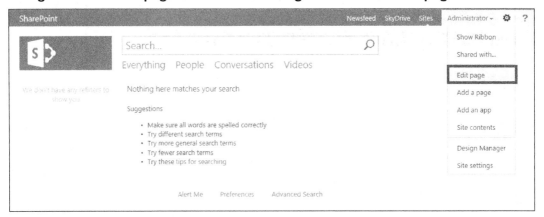

Select Edit Web Part from the Refinement drop-down menu:

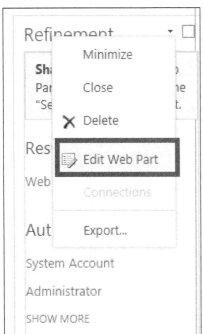

The Refinement web part properties pane is displayed on the right of the page.

The main option in this web part is to configure the refiners for the search results of the given page by clicking the Choose Refiners...button:

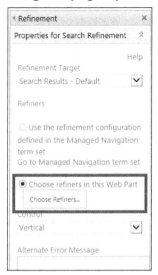

The Refinement configuration dialog appears:

The top section allows you to add or remove refinement properties as well as order them accordingly. The bottom section configures how the refinement is displayed and sorted. Customization of the refinements display and behaviors is covered in the rest of this chapter while the actual configuration of refinement properties is discussed within the bonus chapters.

Adding Search Result Counts to Your Refinements

Overview

The Refinement web part has the ability to display result counts alongside the refinement values for a particular managed property out-of-the-box. However, this option is not available within the web part properties. Enabling search result counts in your refinements requires a tweak within the refinement display templates.

Displaying Counts for All Refinements

The easiest configuration is to simply turn counts on for all refinements. This is achieved by modifying the Filter_Default.html and Filter_MultiValue.html display templates. Using SharePoint Designer 2013, you may access the display templates easily by following the similar steps as outlined in Appendix A.

This time instead of opening the Search sub-folder under Display Templates, open the Filters folder:

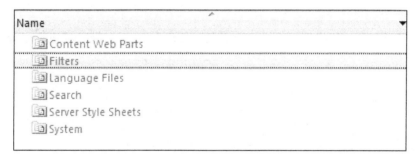

Locate Filter_Default.html. Right-click the file and select Edit File in Advanced Mode:

Inside the code locate the ShowCounts variable and change from false to true:

```
<body>
    <div id="4">
<!--#_

    this.Options = {
        ShowClientPeoplePicker: false,
        ShowCounts: true
    };
```

Save the changes. Your single value refinements now display the counts. Repeat the same process on the Filter_MultiValue.html to display counts on your multi-value refinements.

Displaying Counts for Selective Refinements

There may be situations or search pages where you do not wish to display the refinement counts. For this case, and for best practices sake, it is recommended to make a copy of the Filter templates and create a custom refinement display template accordingly.

Simply right-click the Filter_Default.html file and select Copy:

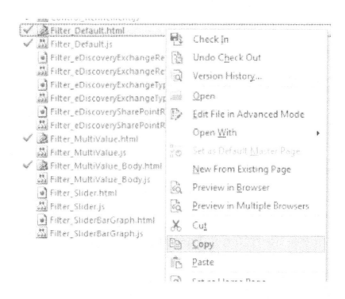

Right-click again and select Paste:

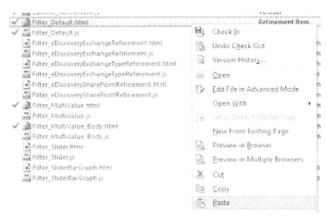

Rename the file accordingly:

Edit the new copied file and change both the Title and ShowCounts values:

Save the changes. Repeat the same process for the Filter_MultiValue.html if desired.

Now when configuring the Refinement web part, when you choose the refiners, your new display template is available in the drop-down:

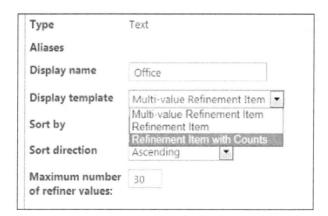

You may now choose to show refinement counts on single and/or multi-value refinement properties:

Office

☐ Palo Alto (13)

☐ Philadelphia (32)

☐ Washington (8)

Instant Refinement of Multi Value Properties

Overview

When you configure a refinement as multi-value, the user is presented with the list of available filters with checkboxes:

The user must select one or more checkboxes and then click on the Apply link. After they click on the Apply link, the results are refined by the selected filters but only the selected filters are presented:

Category

☑ Accessories (29)

☑ Clothing (35)

Other Value

Apply | Clear

With my Instant Refinement solution, all filters are displayed all of the time and when the user clicks on a checkbox, the results are instantly refined without the need to click on an Apply link. This section describes the steps to implement this functionality.

Modify or Copy the Multi Value Display Template

Using SharePoint Designer 2013, navigate to the Filters display templates as explained in the previous section. Copy or modify the Filter_MultiValue.html file. Edit the file in advanced mode.

Store the Original Filters

At the bottom of the display template add the following code to store the original filters:

```
if ($isNull(ctx.RefinementControl["csr_initialFilters"])) {

       ctx.RefinementControl["csr_initialFilters"] = refiners;

}
```

```
ctx["DisplayTemplateData"]["BodyTemplateId"] = "~sitecollection/_cate
ctx.RefinementControl["csr_propertyName"] = propertyName;
ctx.RefinementControl["csr_displayTitle"] = displayTitle;
ctx.RefinementControl["csr_filters"] = refiners;

if ($isNull(ctx.RefinementControl["csr_initialFilters"])) {
    ctx.RefinementControl["csr_initialFilters"] = refiners;
}
```

Retrieve the Original Refiners

Scroll to the top of the display template and create a new array to store the original filters. Also, add logic to retrieve the previous refiners if they exist:

```
var prevRefiners = [];

if (!$isNull(ctx.RefinementControl["csr_initialFilters"])) {

       prevRefiners = ctx.RefinementControl["csr_initialFilters"];
```

```
          listData = prevRefiners;

          hasNoListData = false;

  }
```

```
var propertyName = ctx.RefinementControl.propertyName;
var displayTitle = Srch.Refinement.getRefinementTitle(ctx.RefinementControl);
var isExpanded = Srch.Refinement.getExpanded(ctx.RefinementControl.propertyName);
var useContains = false;
var useKQL = false;
var refiners = [];
var prevRefiners = [];
if (!$isNull(ctx.RefinementControl["csr_initialFilters"])) {
    prevRefiners = ctx.RefinementControl["csr_initialFilters"];
    listData = prevRefiners;
    hasNoListData = false;
}
```

Remove Condition from Refiners Collection Creation

Scroll down the !hasNoListData condition block and remove the !hasAnyFilterTokens &&
check from the condition inside:

```
if(!hasNoListData) {
    for (var i = 0; i < listData.length; i++) {
        var filter = listData[i];
        if(!$isNull(filter)) {
            listDataTokenToDisplayMap[filter.RefinementToken] = filter.RefinementName;
            listDataTokenToCountMap[filter.RefinementToken] = filter.RefinementCount;
            if( hasAnyFilterTokens &&  !$isEmptyString(filter.RefinementName) && !$isEmptyString(filter.RefinementToken)) {
                refiners.push(
                    {
                        RefinementName: filter.RefinementName,
                        RefinementToken: filter.RefinementToken,
                        RefinementCount: filter.RefinementCount,
                        IsSelected: false
                    });
            }
        }
    }
}
```

The resultant condition should now look like this:

```
if(!$isEmptyString(filter.RefinementName) && !$isEmptyString(filter.RefinementToken)) {
    refiners.push(
    {
        RefinementName: filter.RefinementName,
        RefinementToken: filter.RefinementToken,
        RefinementCount: filter.RefinementCount,
        IsSelected: false
    });
}
```

Change Filter Tokens Logic

Scroll down to the hasAnyFilterTokens condition block and remove the refiners.push statement:

```
if(hasAnyFilterTokens) {
    for(var j = 0; j < currentRefinementCategory.get_tokenCount(); j++) {
        var token = currentRefinementCategory.t[j];
        var displayValue = listDataTokenToDisplayMap[token];
        if($isEmptyString(displayValue) && !$isNull(currentRefinementCategory.m)) {
            displayValue = currentRefinementCategory.m[token];
        }
        if(!$isEmptyString(displayValue) && !$isEmptyString(token))
        {
            refiners.push(
            {
                RefinementName: displayValue,
                RefinementToken: token,
                RefinementCount: !$isNull(listDataTokenToCountMap[token]) ? listDataTokenToCountMap[token] : 0,
                IsSelected: true
            });
        }
    }
}
```

Replace with this code:

```
for (var i = 0; i < refiners.length; i++) {

    if (refiners[i].RefinementName == displayValue) {

        refiners[i].IsSelected = true;

    }
```

```
}
```

```
if(!$isEmptyString(displayValue) && !$isEmptyString(token))
{
    for (var i = 0; i < refiners.length; i++) {
        if (refiners[i].RefinementName == displayValue) {
            refiners[i].IsSelected = true;
        }
    }
}
```

Save the file changes.

Modify the Controls in the Body Template

Modify or copy the Filter_MultiValue_Body.html file. Edit the file in advanced mode.

Scroll to the bottom and find the submit link. Copy the onclick property:

```
<div id="SubmitValue">
    <div id="submit">
        <a onclick="Srch.Refinement.submitMultiRefinement('_#= $scriptEncode(propertyName) =#_', $getCli
            href="javascript:{}">
            _#= $htmlEncode($resource('rf_Apply')) =#_
        </a>
```

Paste the onclick into the checkbox inputs:

```
if(isSelected) {

        <input onclick="Srch.Refinement.submitMultiRefinement('_#= $scriptEncode(propertyName)

} else {

        <input onclick="Srch.Refinement.submitMultiRefinement('_#= $scriptEncode(propertyName)

}
```

Now remove the Other and Submit divs sections from the bottom:

```
<div id="OtherValue">
    <div id="_#= $htmlEncode(propertyName + ' SpecifiedValue') =#_">
        <a onclick="Srch.Refinement.multiRefinerSpecifyOtherFilterValue('_#= $scri
           href="javascript:{}">
            _#= $htmlEncode($resource("rf_OtherValue")) =#_
        </a>
    </div>
</div>
<div id="SubmitValue">
    <div id="submit">
        <a onclick="Srch.Refinement.submitMultiRefinement('_#= $scriptEncode(prope
           href="javascript:{}">
            _#= $htmlEncode($resource('rf_Apply')) =#_
        </a>
        |
        <a onclick="$getClientControl(this).updateRefinementFilters('_#= $scriptEn
           href="javascript:{}">
            _#= $htmlEncode($resource('rf_ClearAll')) =#_
        </a>
    </div>
</div>
```

Save the changes to the body file.

Test the Changes

Navigate to your search page that contains the multi value refinements and review the experience:

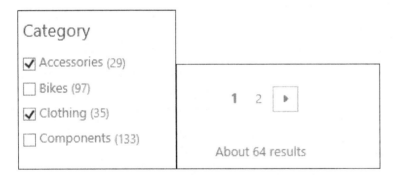

You may click on each checkbox and watch the results instantly refine while always displaying all possible filters.

Cascading Refinement of Multi Value Properties

My cascading refinement solution builds upon the instant refinement solution described in the previous section. The modifications update the result counts in other multi-refinement property sections as well as disables the filters that are no longer available because of the initial refinement.

Store the Property Selected First

Since the cascading is based on the property that is refined first, you must store the property. Scroll to the bottom of the display template file and insert this code:

```
if ($isNull(ctx.ClientControl["PropertySelectedFirst"]) && hasAnyFilterTokens) {

        ctx.ClientControl["PropertySelectedFirst"] = propertyName;

}

else {

        if (ctx.ClientControl["PropertySelectedFirst"] == propertyName && !hasAnyFilterTokens) {

                ctx.ClientControl["PropertySelectedFirst"] = null;

        }

}
```

```
if ($isNull(ctx.RefinementControl["csr_initialFilters"])) {
    ctx.RefinementControl["csr_initialFilters"] = refiners;
}

if ($isNull(ctx.ClientControl["PropertySelectedFirst"]) && hasAnyFilterTokens) {
    ctx.ClientControl["PropertySelectedFirst"] = propertyName;
}
else {
    if (ctx.ClientControl["PropertySelectedFirst"] == propertyName && !hasAnyFilterTokens) {
        ctx.ClientControl["PropertySelectedFirst"] = null;
    }
}
ctx.RefinementControl["csr_isExpanded"] = isExpanded;
ctx.RefinementControl["csr_renderEmptyContainer"] = renderEmptyContainer;
```

Evaluate the List Data and Modify Accordingly

At the top of the file, create a new array to store and process the list data and previous refiners. Add logic to set the list data to the previous refiners:

```
var prevListData = [];
    if (!$isNull(ctx.RefinementControl["csr_initialFilters"])) {
    prevRefiners = ctx.RefinementControl["csr_initialFilters"];
    if (!$isEmptyArray(listData))
    {
                    prevListData = listData;
    }
    listData = prevRefiners;
    hasNoListData = false;
}
```

```
var refiners = [];
var prevRefiners = [];
var prevListData = [];
if (!$isNull(ctx.RefinementControl["csr_initialFilters"])) {
    prevRefiners = ctx.RefinementControl["csr_initialFilters"];
    if (!$isEmptyArray(listData))
    {
        prevListData = listData;
    }
    listData = prevRefiners;
    hasNoListData = false;
}
```

Determine if Filter is Still Available and Update Refinement Count

Within the !hasNoListData condition block, change the refiners.push logic with this code:

```
if (!$isNull(prevListData)) {
                var found = false;
                for (var k = 0; k < prevListData.length; k++) {
                        if (prevListData[k].RefinementName == filter.RefinementName) {
                                found=true;
                                filter.RefinementCount = prevList-
Data[k].RefinementCount;
                        }
                }
}
                refiners.push(
                {
                RefinementName: filter.RefinementName,
                RefinementToken: filter.RefinementToken,
                RefinementCount: filter.RefinementCount,
                IsSelected: false,
                WasFound: Boolean(found),
                IsDisabled: false
```

```
                    });
    ... ... .. ........................  ..,.
if(!hasNoListData) {
    for (var i = 0; i < listData.length; i++) {
        var filter = listData[i];
        if(!$isNull(filter)) {
            listDataTokenToDisplayMap[filter.RefinementToken] = filter.RefinementName;
            listDataTokenToCountMap[filter.RefinementToken] = filter.RefinementCount;
            if(!$isEmptyString(filter.RefinementName) && !$isEmptyString(filter.RefinementToken)) {

                if (!$isNull(prevListData)) {
                    var found = false;
                    for (var k = 0; k < prevListData.length; k++) {
                        if (prevListData[k].RefinementName == filter.RefinementName) {
                            found=true;
                            filter.RefinementCount = prevListData[k].RefinementCount;
                        }
                    }
                }
                refiners.push(
                {
                    RefinementName: filter.RefinementName,
                    RefinementToken: filter.RefinementToken,
                    RefinementCount: filter.RefinementCount,
                    IsSelected: false,
                    WasFound: Boolean(found),
                    IsDisabled: false
                });
            }

        }
    }
```

Flag Filters that Should Be Disabled

Flagging the filters that should be disabled involves two modifications. The first is to add the following code within the hasFilterTokens condition:

```
if (!$isNull(ctx.ClientControl["PropertySelectedFirst"]) &&
ctx.ClientControl["PropertySelectedFirst"] != propertyName) {

        for (var i = 0; i < refiners.length; i++) {

            if (!refiners[i].WasFound) {

                refiners[i].IsDisabled = true;

                refiners[i].RefinementCount = 0;

            }
```

```
        }
    }

if(hasAnyFilterTokens) {
    for(var j = 0; j < currentRefinementCategory.get_tokenCount(); j++) {
        var token = currentRefinementCategory.t[j];
        var displayValue = listDataTokenToDisplayMap[token];
        if($isEmptyString(displayValue) && !$isNull(currentRefinementCategory.m)) {
            displayValue = currentRefinementCategory.m[token];
        }
        if(!$isEmptyString(displayValue) && !$isEmptyString(token))
        {
            for (var i = 0; i < refiners.length; i++) {
                if (refiners[i].RefinementName == displayValue) {
                    refiners[i].IsSelected = true;
                }
            }
        }
    }
    if (!$isNull(ctx.ClientControl["PropertySelectedFirst"]) && ctx.ClientControl["PropertySelectedFirst"] != propertyName) {
        for (var i = 0; i < refiners.length; i++) {
            if (!refiners[i].WasFound) {
                refiners[i].IsDisabled = true;
            }
        }
    }
}
else
{
    if (!$isNull(ctx.RefinementControl["csr_initialFilters"])) {
        for (var i = 0; i < refiners.length; i++) {
            if (!refiners[i].WasFound) {
                refiners[i].IsDisabled = true;
                refiners[i].RefinementCount = 0;
            }
        }
    }
}
```

The second portion involves adding an else condition to the hasFIlterTokens if statement:

```
else {

    if (!$isNull(ctx.RefinementControl["csr_initialFilters"])) {

        for (var i = 0; i < refiners.length; i++) {

            if (!refiners[i].WasFound) {

                refiners[i].IsDisabled = true;

                refiners[i].RefinementCount = 0;

            }

        }
```

```
   }}
```

Save the changes to the file.

Modify the Body Display Template

Within the for-loop, create an isDisabled variable and a fontWeight variable:

```
for (var i = 0; i < filters.length; i++){
    var filter = filters[i];
    if(!$isNull(filter)){
        var isSelected = Boolean(filter.IsSelected);
        var isDisabled = Boolean(filter.IsDisabled);
        var inputName = propertyName + '_ChkGroup';
        var inputId = inputName + "_" + filter.RefinementName;
        var nameClass = "ms-ref-name " + (showCounts ? "ms-displayInline" :
        var fontWeight = "normal";
```

In the isSelected if statement, add fontweight="bold"; :

```
if(isSelected) {
    fontWeight = "bold";

        <input type="checkbox" onclick="Srch.Refinement.

}
```

Now, branch the else statement to check for isDisabled:

```
else {
    if (isDisabled) {
        fontWeight = "200";

        <input type="checkbox" disabled="disabled" onclick="Srch.Refinement.s

    }
    else {

        <input type="checkbox" onclick="Srch.Refinement.submitMultiRefinement(

    }
}
```

For the disabled version, just copy the input for the unselected check box but add the disabled="disabled" property.

Finally in the label, add the following style property using the fontWeight variable:

style="font-weight:_#= fontWeight =#_"

```
<label style="font-weight:_#= fontWeight =#_"
_#= $htmlEncode(filter.RefinementName) =#_
```

Save the changes to the body file.

Test the Cascade Functionality

Navigate to the search results page that contains the multi value refinements:

Category

- ☐ Accessories (29)
- ☐ Bikes (97)
- ☐ Clothing (35)
- ☐ Components (133)

Sub Category

- ☐ Bib-Shorts (3)
- ☐ Bike Racks (1)
- ☐ Bike Stands (1)
- ☐ Bottles, Holders, and Cages (3)
- ☐ Bottom Bicycle Bracketss (3)
- ☐ Brakes (1)
- ☐ Caps (1)
- ☐ Chains (1)
- ☐ Cleaners (1)
- ☐ Cranksets (3)
- ☐ Derailleurs (2)

Click on one of the filters.

Category

☑ **Accessories** (29) ⟵━━━ **Selected filters are bolded and checked**

☐ Bikes (97)

☐ Clothing (35)

☐ Components (133)

Sub Category

☐ Bib-Shorts (0)

☐ Bike Racks (1)

☐ Bike Stands (1)

☐ Bottles, Holders, and Cages (3)

☐ Bottom Bicycle Bracketss (0)

☐ Brakes (0)

☐ Caps (0)

☐ Chains (0)

☐ Cleaners (1)

Available filters are updated with refined counts

Unavailable filters are now disabled

THIS PAGE INTENTIONALLY BLANK

End-to-End Solution: Enhancing the Search Center UX with a Custom Vertical

This bonus chapter demonstrates the creation of a custom result type using the query builder to define the items to include. The scenario is that Human Resources (HR) produces and maintains policy documents in PDF format. These documents are stored all within a particular location on the HR department site. Users need to be able to search within Policies and have the appropriate results display. Creating a new search results page and adding it to the search navigation is also

Create a Custom Result Source

Navigate to your Search Center and select Site Settings from the Settings menu:

Under the Site Collection Administration section, click on Search Result Sources:

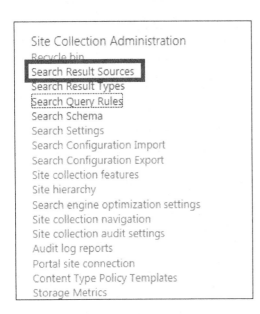

On the Manage Result Sources page, click on the New Result Source link:

Site Collection Administration › Manage Result Sources

Use result sources to scope search results and federate queries to external sources, such as internet search engines. After defining a rule actions to use it. Learn more about result sources.

Result Sources replace Search Scopes, which are now deprecated. You can still view your old scopes and use them in queries, but n

New Result Source

On the Add Result Source page, enter a name for the Result Source. For this example, I am using Policies:

MorganNet Search Center

Site Collection Administration › Add Result Source

(i) **Note:** This result source will be available to all sites in the site collection. To make one for just this site, use site result source.

General Information

Names must be unique at each administrative level. For example, two result sources in a site cannot share a name, but one in a site and one provided by the site collection can.

Descriptions are shown as tooltips when selecting result sources in other configuration pages.

Name

Policies

Description

Protocol

Select Local SharePoint for results from the index of this Search Service.

Select OpenSearch 1.0/1.1 for results from a search engine that uses that protocol.

Select Exchange for results from an exchange source.

◉ Local SharePoint
◯ Remote SharePoint
◯ OpenSearch 1.0/1.1
◯ Exchange

Scroll down and click on the Launch Query Builder button:

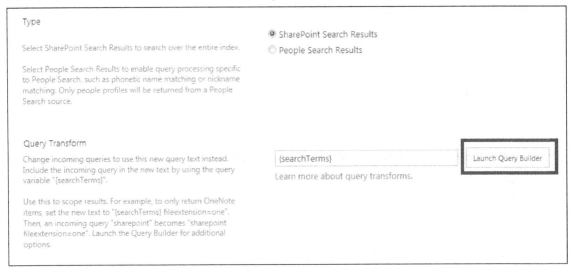

In the Property Filter section, select Path, Contains, and Manual value in the respective drop-downs:

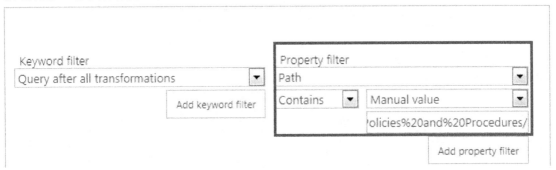

Enter in the path of where the policy documents are located (e.g. http://spname/sites/HR/Policies/) and click Add property filter:

The property filter is added to the Query text. You may optionally add a FileType filter such as shown above in the Query text.

NOTE: The URL must be http encoded, so for example, spaces need to be represented by %20. It is easier if you navigate to the location and copy the URL location from the browser. Also, you would think that "Starts with" is a better choice than "Contains" but for some reason with the Path property, the "Starts with" option was not returning any results.

Click OK on the Build Your Query dialog.

The property filter is added to the Query Transform text box.

Click Save:

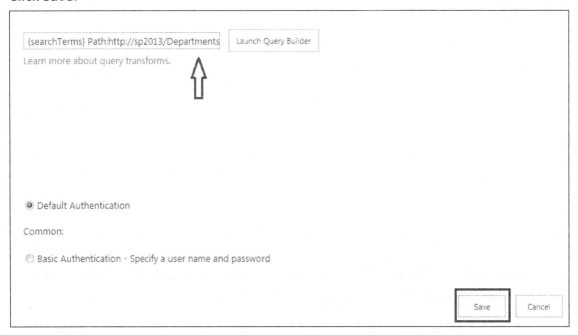

Create a Custom Result Type for the Custom Result Source

Navigate to your Search Center and select Site Settings from the Settings menu.

Under the Site Collection Administration section, click on the Search Result Types link:

Site Collection Administration
Recycle bin
Search Result Sources
Search Result Types
Search Query Rules
Search Schema
Search Settings
Search Configuration Import
Search Configuration Export
Site collection features
Site hierarchy
Search engine optimization settings
Site collection navigation

On the Result Types page click on the New Result Type link:

Search Center

Site Collection Administration

Tailor the look of important result types by crafting a display template in HTML and defining a rule tha
priority. Learn more about how to configure result types.

New Result Type

Enter a name for the Result Type. Select the Result Source created in the previous section from the source drop-down. In this example, all Policy documents are PDF so the content and display templates are the PDF options:

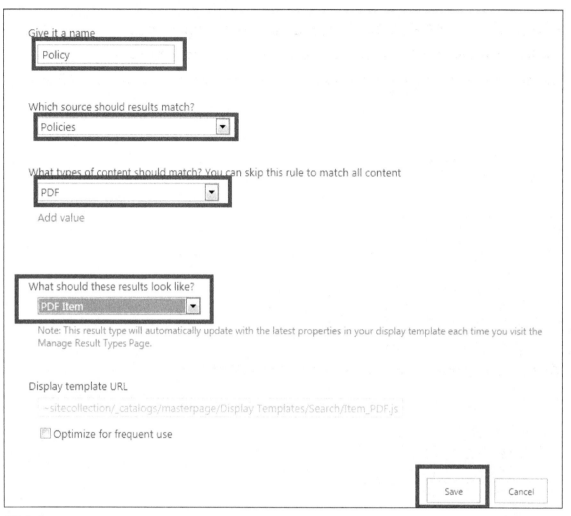

Click Save.

Create a Custom Results Page for the Custom Result Type

Navigate to your Search Center and select Site Contents from the Settings menu:

Locate and double-click the Pages library:

From the Files tab in the top ribbon, select Page from the New Document drop-down menu:

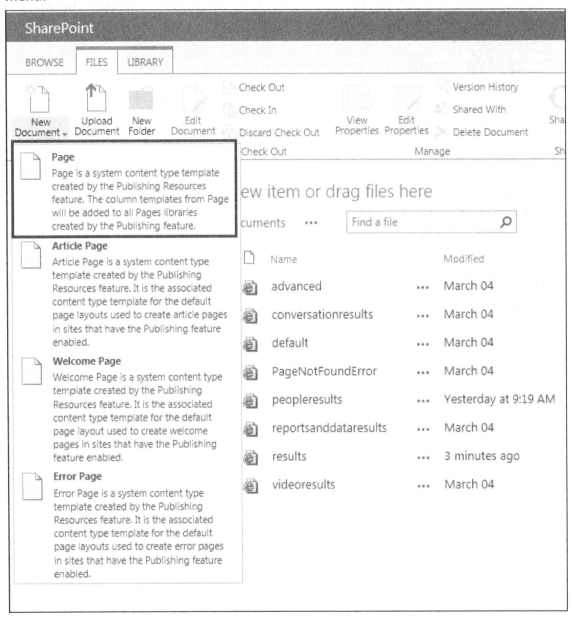

On the Create Page page, enter a title and URL Name. Click Create.

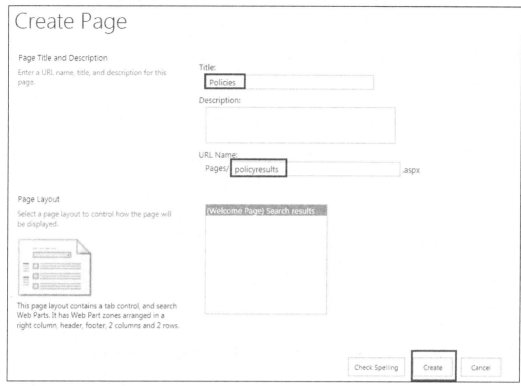

Select the ellipsis menu on the new page and click on OPEN:

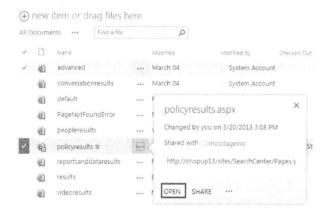

From the Settings menu select Edit page:

Locate the Search Results web part and select Edit Web Part from the drop-down menu:

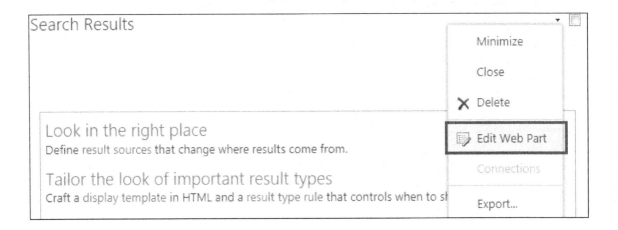

In the Properties tool pane that appeared on the right, click the Change query button:

The Build Your Query dialog appears.

In the Select a query section, select the custom Result Source created in the first section of this chapter:

Build Your Query

BASICS   REFINERS   SORTING   SETTINGS   TEST

Switch to Quick Mode

Select a query
Choose what content you want to search by
selecting a result source.

| Policies (Site Collection) | ▼ |

Keyword filter

| Query from the search box | ▼ |

Add keyword filter

Property filter

| Select property | ▼ |
| Contains | ▼ | Select value | ▼ |

Add property filter

Click OK on the Build Your Query dialog.

Click OK in the web part properties tool pane:

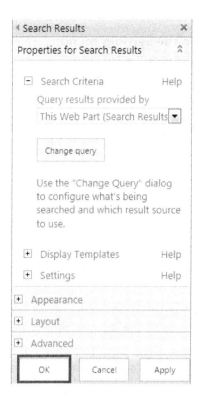

Check in the page:

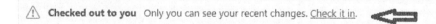

Publish the page:

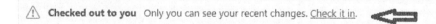

Add a Custom Results Page to the Search Center Navigation

Navigate to your Search Center and select Site Settings from the Settings menu:

Under the Search section click the Search Settings link:

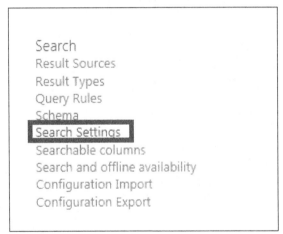

At the bottom the Search Settings page, click on Add Link...:

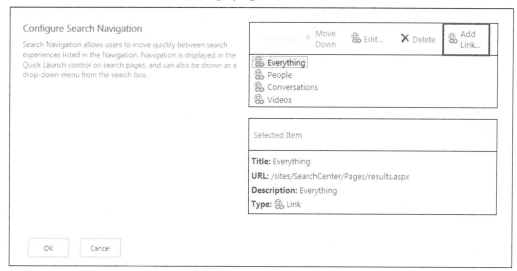

Enter a title and the URL to the custom page that was created in the previous section. Click OK.

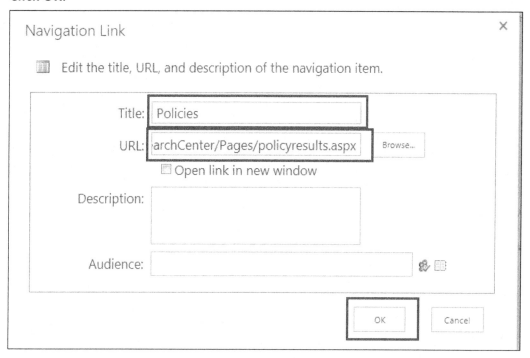

Back on the Search Settings page click OK:

Configure Search Navigation

Search Navigation allows users to move quickly between search experiences listed in the Navigation. Navigation is displayed in the Quick Launch control on search pages, and can also be shown as a drop-down menu from the search box.

⬆ Move Up   🔗 Edit...   ✖ Delete   🔗 Add Link...

🔗 Everything
🔗 People
🔗 Conversations
🔗 Videos
🔗 Policies

Selected Item

Title: Policies
URL: /sites/SearchCenter/Pages/policyresults.aspx
Description:
Type: 🔗 Link

OK   Cancel

Test the Results

Navigate to your Search Center. The new navigation item appears at the top. Click on the new link and perform a search:

End-to-End Solution: Incorporating External Data using BCS into the Search Center UX

This chapter demonstrates an end-to-end solution incorporating customer data into your Search Center experience. The Business Data Connectivity Service is used to produce an external content type based on a customer database.

Prepare the Data Source

The scenario and sample data for this chapter uses Product information from the AdventureWorks2012 sample database in SQL Server.

The first step is to create your read list and read item procedures.

Create a stored procedure that returns all of the information you want to search and make sure all rows are returned:

```
CREATE PROCEDURE GetAllProductsForBCS
AS
BEGIN
    -- SET NOCOUNT ON added to prevent extra result sets from
    -- interfering with SELECT statements.
    SET NOCOUNT ON;

    -- Insert statements for procedure here
    SELECT
        p.ProductID,
        p.ProductNumber,
        p.Name AS ProductName,
        p.Class AS ProductClass,
        p.Color AS ProductColor,
        p.ProductLine,
        p.ListPrice AS ProductListPrice,
        pc.Name AS ProductCategory,
        psc.Name AS ProductSubCategory,
        pm.Name AS ProductModel,
        pd.Description as ProductDescription
    FROM Production.Product p
```

100 %   <

	ProductID	ProductNumber	ProductName	ProductClass	ProductColor	ProductLine	ProductListPrice	ProductCategory	ProductSubCategory	ProductModel	ProductDescription
1	994	BB-7421	LL Bottom Bracket	L	NULL	NULL	53.99	Components	Bottom Brackets	LL Bottom Bracket	Chromoly steel.
2	995	BB-8107	ML Bottom Bracket	M	NULL	NULL	101.24	Components	Bottom Brackets	ML Bottom Bracket	Aluminum alloy cups; large d
3	996	BB-9108	HL Bottom Bracket	H	NULL	NULL	121.49	Components	Bottom Brackets	HL Bottom Bracket	Aluminum alloy cups and a h
4	984	BK-M18S-40	Mountain-500 Silver, 40	L	Silver	M	564.99	Bikes	Mountain Bikes	Mountain-500	Suitable for any type of riding
5	985	BK-M18S-42	Mountain-500 Silver, 42	L	Silver	M	564.99	Bikes	Mountain Bikes	Mountain-500	Suitable for any type of riding
6	986	BK-M18S-44	Mountain-500 Silver, 44	L	Silver	M	564.99	Bikes	Mountain Bikes	Mountain-500	Suitable for any type of riding
7	987	BK-M18S-48	Mountain-500 Silver, 48	L	Silver	M	564.99	Bikes	Mountain Bikes	Mountain-500	Suitable for any type of riding
8	988	BK-M18S-52	Mountain-500 Silver, 52	L	Silver	M	564.99	Bikes	Mountain Bikes	Mountain-500	Suitable for any type of riding
9	989	BK-M18B-40	Mountain-500 Black, 40	L	Black	M	539.99	Bikes	Mountain Bikes	Mountain-500	Suitable for any type of riding
10	990	BK-M18B-42	Mountain-500 Black, 42	L	Black	M	539.99	Bikes	Mountain Bikes	Mountain-500	Suitable for any type of riding
11	991	BK-M18B-44	Mountain-500 Black, 44	L	Black	M	539.99	Bikes	Mountain Bikes	Mountain-500	Suitable for any type of riding
12	992	BK-M18B-48	Mountain-500 Black, 48	L	Black	M	539.99	Bikes	Mountain Bikes	Mountain-500	Suitable for any type of riding
13	993	BK-M18B-52	Mountain-500 Black, 52	L	Black	M	539.99	Bikes	Mountain Bikes	Mountain-500	Suitable for any type of riding
14	980	BK-M38S-38	Mountain-400-W Silver, 38	M	Silver	M	769.49	Bikes	Mountain Bikes	Mountain-400-W	This bike delivers a high-leve

I created a GetAllProductsForBCS stored procedure which returns the product information I need using several joins:

```sql
CREATE PROCEDURE GetAllProductsForBCS
AS
BEGIN
        -- SET NOCOUNT ON added to prevent extra result sets from
        -- interfering with SELECT statements.
        SET NOCOUNT ON;

    -- Insert statements for procedure here
        SELECT
                p.ProductID,
                p.ProductNumber,
                p.Name AS ProductName,
                p.Class AS ProductClass,
                p.Color AS ProductColor,
                p.ProductLine,
                p.ListPrice AS ProductListPrice,
                pc.Name AS ProductCategory,
                psc.Name AS ProductSubCategory,
                pm.Name AS ProductModel,
                pd.Description as ProductDescription
        FROM Production.Product p
                INNER JOIN Production.ProductSubcategory psc
                    ON psc.ProductSubcategoryID = p.ProductSubcategoryID
                INNER JOIN Production.ProductCategory pc
                    ON pc.ProductCategoryID = psc.ProductCategoryID
                INNER JOIN Production.ProductModel pm
                    on pm.ProductModelID = p.ProductModelID
                 INNER JOIN Production.ProductModelProductDescriptionCulture pmx
                    ON pm.ProductModelID = pmx.ProductModelID
                INNER JOIN Production.ProductDescription pd
                    ON pmx.ProductDescriptionID = pd.ProductDescriptionID
        WHERE pmx.CultureID='en'
```

This procedure is used to create a ReadList method in the External Content Type.

Create a stored procedure that returns the same information but only for a particular entity by using the ID as a parameter:

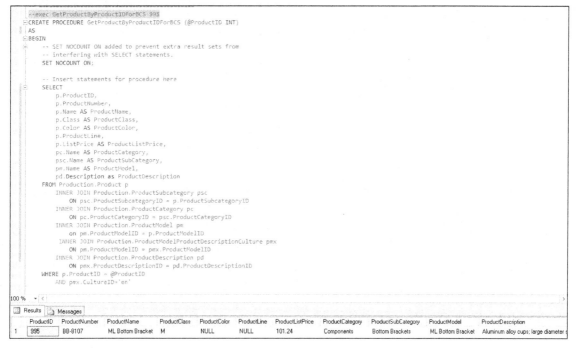

```sql
--exec GetProductByProductIDForBCS 995
CREATE PROCEDURE GetProductByProductIDForBCS (@ProductID INT)
AS
BEGIN
    -- SET NOCOUNT ON added to prevent extra result sets from
    -- interfering with SELECT statements.
    SET NOCOUNT ON;

    -- Insert statements for procedure here
    SELECT
        p.ProductID,
        p.ProductNumber,
        p.Name AS ProductName,
        p.Class AS ProductClass,
        p.Color AS ProductColor,
        p.ProductLine,
        p.ListPrice AS ProductListPrice,
        pc.Name AS ProductCategory,
        psc.Name AS ProductSubCategory,
        pm.Name AS ProductModel,
        pd.Description as ProductDescription
    FROM Production.Product p
        INNER JOIN Production.ProductSubcategory psc
            ON psc.ProductSubcategoryID = p.ProductSubcategoryID
        INNER JOIN Production.ProductCategory pc
            ON pc.ProductCategoryID = psc.ProductCategoryID
        INNER JOIN Production.ProductModel pm
            on pm.ProductModelID = p.ProductModelID
        INNER JOIN Production.ProductModelProductDescriptionCulture pmx
            ON pm.ProductModelID = pmx.ProductModelID
        INNER JOIN Production.ProductDescription pd
            ON pmx.ProductDescriptionID = pd.ProductDescriptionID
    WHERE p.ProductID = @ProductID
        AND pmx.CultureID='en'
```

	ProductID	ProductNumber	ProductName	ProductClass	ProductColor	ProductLine	ProductListPrice	ProductCategory	ProductSubCategory	ProductModel	ProductDescription
1	995	BB-8107	ML Bottom Bracket	M	NULL	NULL	101.24	Components	Bottom Brackets	ML Bottom Bracket	Aluminum alloy cups; large diameter

Make sure only 1 row is returned for a given identity.

I created a GetAllProductsForBCS stored procedure which returns the product information I need based on the passed in ProductID parameter:

```
CREATE PROCEDURE GetProductByProductIDForBCS (@ProductID INT)
AS
BEGIN
        -- SET NOCOUNT ON added to prevent extra result sets from
        -- interfering with SELECT statements.
        SET NOCOUNT ON;

    -- Insert statements for procedure here
        SELECT
                p.ProductID,
                p.ProductNumber,
                p.Name AS ProductName,
                p.Class AS ProductClass,
                p.Color AS ProductColor,
                p.ProductLine,
                p.ListPrice AS ProductListPrice,
                pc.Name AS ProductCategory,
                psc.Name AS ProductSubCategory,
                pm.Name AS ProductModel,
                pd.Description as ProductDescription
        FROM Production.Product p
                INNER JOIN Production.ProductSubcategory psc
                        ON psc.ProductSubcategoryID = p.ProductSubcategoryID
                INNER JOIN Production.ProductCategory pc
                        ON pc.ProductCategoryID = psc.ProductCategoryID
                INNER JOIN Production.ProductModel pm
                        on pm.ProductModelID = p.ProductModelID
                 INNER JOIN Production.ProductModelProductDescriptionCulture pmx
                        ON pm.ProductModelID = pmx.ProductModelID
                INNER JOIN Production.ProductDescription pd
                        ON pmx.ProductDescriptionID = pd.ProductDescriptionID
        WHERE p.ProductID = @ProductID
                AND pmx.CultureID='en'
```

This procedure is used to create a ReadItem method in the External Content Type. The SELECT statement here should be exactly the same as the SELECT in the ReadList. The only difference here is that additional WHERE condition for the passed in @ProductID.

Add Credentials to the Secure Store Service

In order for the External Content Type to be created and BCS to access your external data source, the data source credentials need to be stored. The Secure Store Service in SharePoint allows you to store credentials. For this scenario, a SQL database account was created named "AWDBAccount". Therefore an entry in the Secure Store Service needs to be added for SQL Authentication.

Navigate to Central Administration and click on Manage Service Applications under the Application Management section:

Click on the Secure Store Service application link:

Search Administration Web Service for Search Service Application

Search Service Application

   Search Service Application Proxy

Secure Store Service

   Secure Store Service

Security Token Service Application

User Profile App

   User Profile App

WSS_UsageApplication

   WSS_UsageApplication

If you do not have a Secure Store Service listed, you'll need to create one.

If you see a message at the top of the screen regarding a key, click the Generate New Key button from the top ribbon:

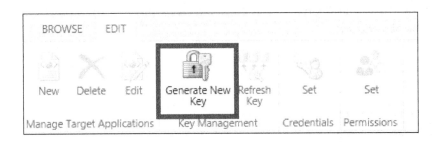

Enter a pass phrase and click OK:

Click New from the top ribbon:

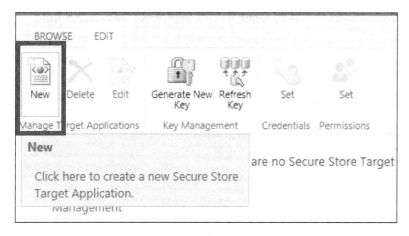

Enter a Target Application ID, Display Name, and Contact E-mail:

You will need the Target Application ID to create the External Content Type. **Click Next.**

Change the Windows User Name field name to User ID the Windows Password field name to Password.

Change the associated Field Types from to User Name and Password. Click Next.

Enter Target Application Administrators and click OK:

The Target Application entry is created:

Select the Target Application checkbox and click the Set Credentials button:

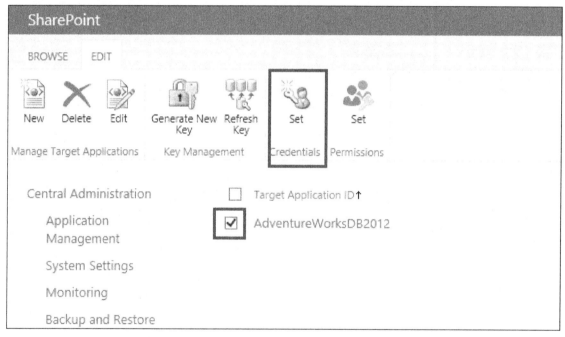

Enter the Credential Owner (this should be the service account that runs BCS), enter the SQL database User ID and Password. Click OK:

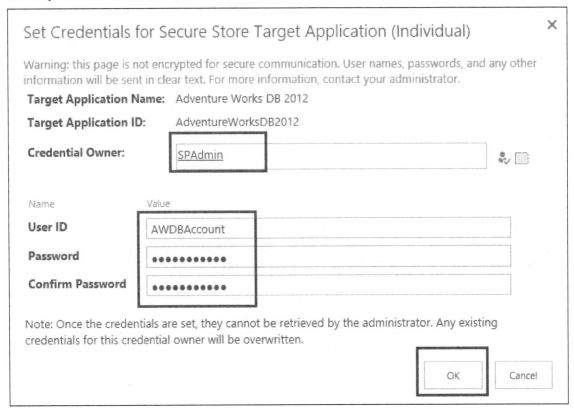

Create an External Content Type

The methods here describe the steps for a no-code solution in creating an External Content Type that uses your data source as the provider of information via SharePoint Designer 2013.

Launch SharePoint Designer 2013 and open your Search Center site:

Click the External Content Types from the Site Objects and then click the External Content Type button from the top-ribbon:

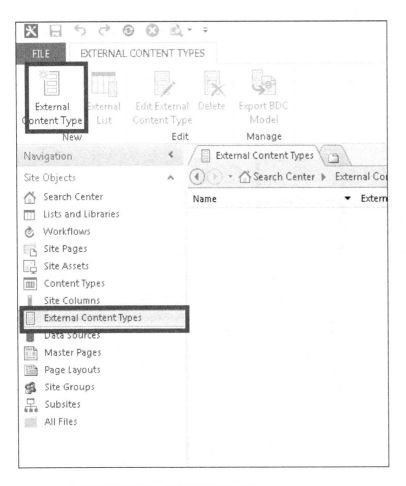

Enter a Name and Display Name and then click on the External System link:

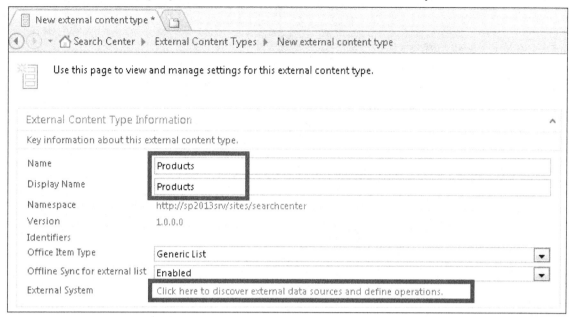

Click on the Add Connection button:

Select the type of connection. For this example, SQL Server is being used:

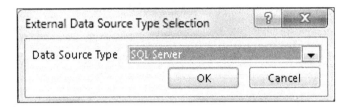

Click OK.

Enter the Database Server, the Database Name, and select Connect with Impersonated Custom Identity. Enter the Secure Store Application ID that was created in the previous section:

SQL Server Connection

Connection Properties

Database Server: SQLSRV2012

Database Name: AdventureWorks2012

Name (optional): Adventure Works 2012

○ Connect with User's Identity

○ Connect with Impersonated Windows Identity

● Connect with Impersonated Custom Identity

Secure Store Application ID: AdventureWorksDB2012

OK   Cancel

Click OK.

If prompted, enter SQL Server credentials to access the database.

Expand the database in the Data Source Explorer tab and then expand the Routines folder. Locate the Read List procedure, right click and select New Read List Operation:

Enter an Operation Name and Display Name.

The Operation Name becomes a prefix (ReadList.propertyname) in the crawled properties so it is a good idea to include an entity description in the name, otherwise it would be hard to distinguish crawled properties from their external content types.

Click Next.

The example does not limit the Read List items and thus there are no Input Parameters.
Click Next:

On the Return Parameter Configuration screen, make sure the row identifier (primary key) is selected and check the Map to Identifier checkbox. The Identifier, Field, and DisplayName become populated with the row identifier. **Click Finish.**

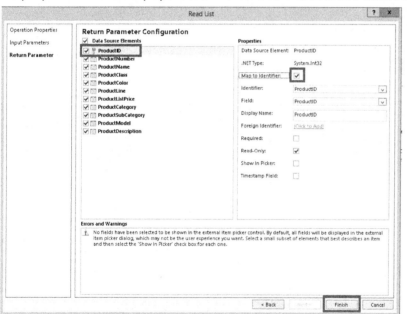

Next, locate the Read Item procedure, right click and select New Read Item Operation:

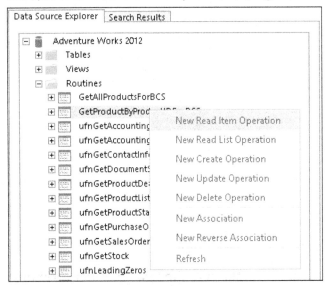

Enter appropriate operation names. Click Next:

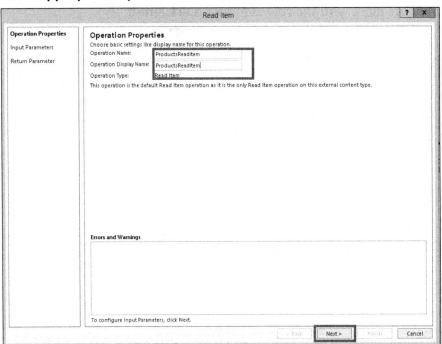

On the Input Parameters Configuration screen, make sure the input parameter is selected and the Map to Identifier is checked. Click Next:

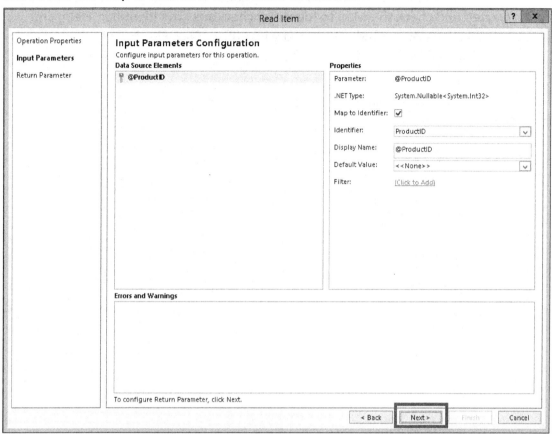

On the Return Parameter Configuration screen, make sure the row identifier (primary key) is selected and check the Map to Identifier checkbox. The Identifier, Field, and DisplayName become populated with the row identifier. **Click Finish.**

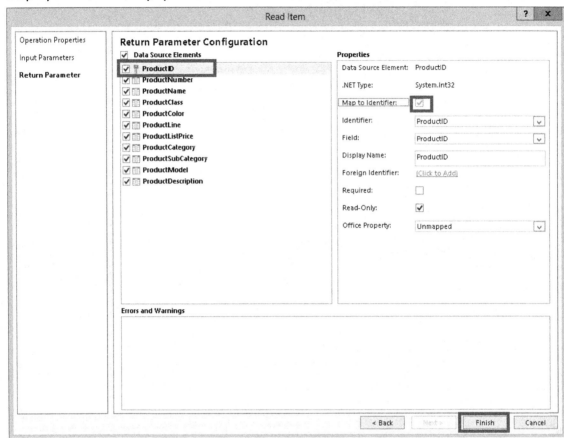

The new operations appear in the External Content Type Operations section:

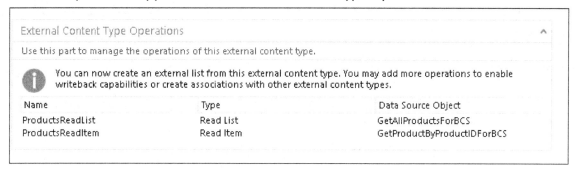

Save the External Content Type:

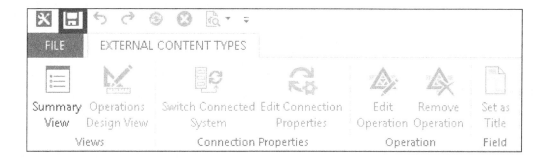

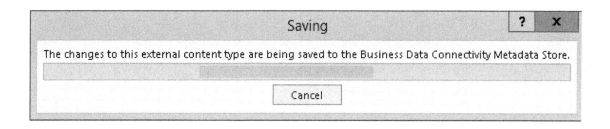

Keep SharePoint Designer 2013 open to the External Content Type. Navigate to your Business Data Connectivity Service Application and verify the new external content type exists:

In your Business Data Connectivity Service Application, click the Configure button:

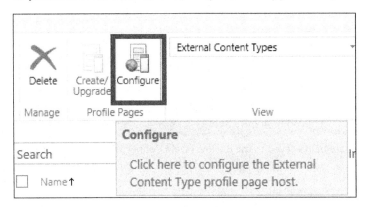

Enter a location to host the External Content Type profile pages:

Configure External Content Type Profile Page Host

Configure External Content
Type Profile Page Host

Specify a SharePoint site where
profile pages of External
Content Types will be created.
You can update this site at any
time. But we strongly
recommend you use a single,
dedicated SharePoint site to
host the profile pages of all your
External Content Types.

☑ Enable Profile Page Creation
Host SharePoint site URL (e.g.
http://www.contoso.com/sitename)

http://sp2013srv/sites/searchcenter

It is recommended to use a dedicate SharePoint site. I personally like things being all together in my Search Center Site Collection so I use that.

Scroll down and click OK.

While you are here you could set the permissions in the BCS for the External Content type as explained in the next section (or just come back to it).

Navigate back to SharePoint Designer 2013 and with the External Content Type opened, click on the Create Profile Page button from the top-ribbon:

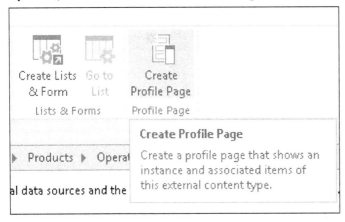

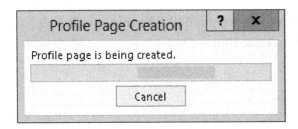

The Profile Page is created. This page becomes used for the search results URL if a custom URL (page) is not used as part of the data source.

Set Permissions on the BCS Entity

Navigate to your Business Data Connectivity Service Application and select the External Content Type by checking the checkbox:

Click on the Set Object Permissions button from the top-ribbon.

Enter accounts into the account box (if your external content type is for general use include Everyone):

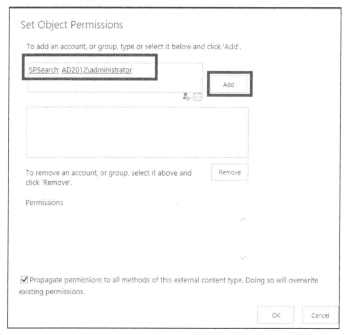

Click Add. Select each added account and check off the appropriate permissions. For Everyone, only check off Execute and Selectable In Clients.

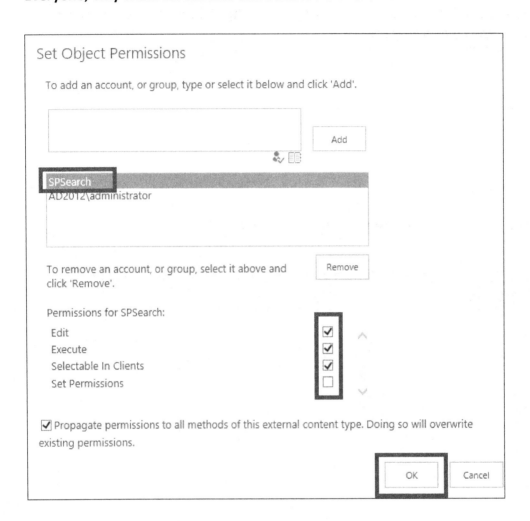

Click OK.

Create a Content Source for the External Content Type

Navigate to Central Administration and click on Manage service applications:

Click on the Search Service Application:

Click on Content Sources under Crawling (in the left hand column):

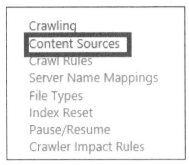

On the Manage Content Source page click the New Content Source link:

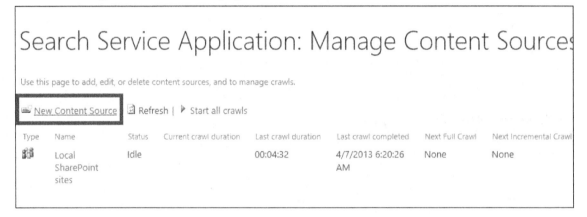

Enter a name for the Content Source and select Line of Business Data. Select the Crawl selected external data source and check off the data source:

Name: *

Products

Select the type of content to be crawled:

○ SharePoint Sites
○ Web Sites
○ File Shares
○ Exchange Public Folders
◉ Line of Business Data
○ Custom Repository

Select the Business Data Connectivity Service Application:

Business Data Connectivity ▼

○ Crawl all external data sources in this Business Data Connectivity Service Application
◉ Crawl selected external data source
☑ Adventure Works 2012

Scroll down and click OK.

The content source is created and listed on the Manage Content Sources page:

Search Service Application: Manage Content Sources

Use this page to add, edit, or delete content sources, and to manage crawls.

📄 New Content Source | 🔃 Refresh | ▶ Start all crawls

Type	Name	Status	Current crawl duration	Last crawl duration	Last crawl completed	Next Full Crawl	Next Incremental Crawl	Priority
🗐	Local SharePoint sites	Idle		00:04:32	4/7/2013 6:20:26 AM	None	None	Normal
🗐	Products	Idle				None	None	Normal

Hover over the new content source and click the drop-down menu. Select Start Full Crawl:

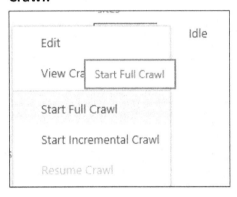

Create Managed Properties Based on Crawled Properties

After the crawl has completed, you now need to create managed properties and map them to the crawled properties from the new content source. This may be accomplished from the Search Service Application UI or from PowerShell. Either way, you need to know what crawled properties have been created.

From the Search Service Application, click on Search Schema on the left hand side of the screen under Queries and Results:

Queries and Results
Authoritative Pages
Result Sources
Query Rules
Query Client Types
Search Schema
Query Suggestions
Search Dictionaries
Search Result Removal

On the Managed Properties page, click on Crawled Properties at the top:

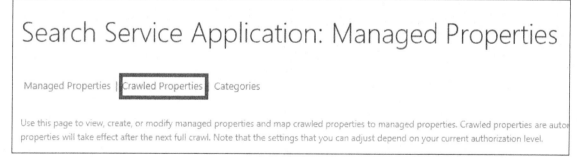

Search Service Application: Managed Properties

Managed Properties | Crawled Properties | Categories

Use this page to view, create, or modify managed properties and map crawled properties to managed properties. Crawled properties are autor properties will take effect after the next full crawl. Note that the settings that you can adjust depend on your current authorization level.

Select Business Data from the Category drop-down and click the filter button:

The crawled properties from the external data source are displayed:

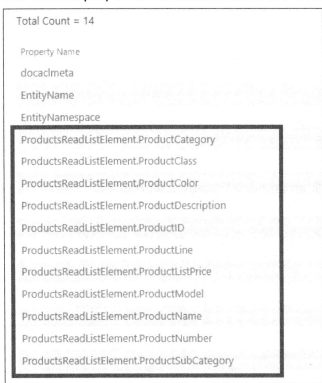

You may also use PowerShell to list out the crawled properties. I use the following commands:

Add-PSSnapin Microsoft.SharePoint.PowerShell -ErrorAction SilentlyContinue

$ssa = Get-SPEnterpriseSearchServiceApplication

Get-SPEnterpriseSearchMetadataCrawledProperty -SearchApplication $ssa -Category 'Business Data' | ft Name

```
Administrator: Windows PowerShell                                    _  □  x

PS C:\> Add-PSSnapin Microsoft.SharePoint.PowerShell -ErrorAction SilentlyContinue
PS C:\>
PS C:\> $ssa = Get-SPEnterpriseSearchServiceApplication
PS C:\>
PS C:\>
PS C:\> Get-SPEnterpriseSearchMetadataCrawledProperty -SearchApplication $ssa -Category 'Business Data' | ft Name

Name
----
docaclmeta
EntityName
EntityNamespace
ProductsReadListElement.ProductCategory
ProductsReadListElement.ProductClass
ProductsReadListElement.ProductColor
ProductsReadListElement.ProductDescription
ProductsReadListElement.ProductID
ProductsReadListElement.ProductLine
ProductsReadListElement.ProductListPrice
ProductsReadListElement.ProductModel
ProductsReadListElement.ProductName
ProductsReadListElement.ProductNumber
ProductsReadListElement.ProductSubCategory


PS C:\> _
```

Now that you know what the crawled properties are, you can map them to managed properties. If the managed properties were already created, you could simply click on each crawled property on the Crawled Property page and map them. In this case, there are no managed properties yet.

Therefore click on the Managed Properties link at the top of the Crawled Properties page:

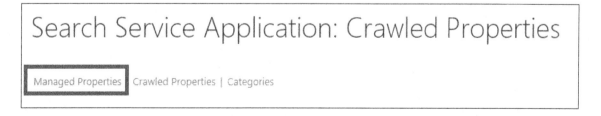

Search Service Application: Crawled Properties

Managed Properties | Crawled Properties | Categories

On the Managed Properties page, click on New Managed Property:

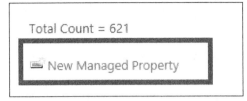

Enter a name for the property. I usually prefix them with the entity type so they are all displayed together and I know which content source they are from. Select the Type and check the Searchable checkbox:

Property name:

ProductCategory

Description:

The type of information in this property:

◉ Text

○ Integer

○ Decimal

○ Date and Time

○ Yes/No

○ Double precision float

○ Binary

☑ Searchable

Scroll down and check Queryable and Retrievable. For this example, the Product Cate-gory will be refinable and sortable so I selected "Yes -active" for both of those entries:

Queryable:
Enables querying against the specific managed
property. The managed property field name
must be included in the query, either specified
in the query itself or included in the query
programmatically. If the managed property is
"author", the query must contain
"author:Smith".

☑ Queryable

Retrievable:
Enables the content of this managed property
to be returned in search results. Enable this
setting for managed properties that are
relevant to present in search results.

☑ Retrievable

Allow multiple values:
Allow multiple values of the same type in this
managed property. For example, if this is the
"author" managed property, and a document
has multiple authors, each author name will be
stored as a separate value in this managed
property.

☐ Allow multiple values

Refinable:
Yes - active: Enables using the property as a
refiner for search results in the front end. You
must manually configure the refiner in the web
part.
Yes - latent: Enables switching refinable to
active later, without having to do a full re-crawl
when you switch.
Both options require a full crawl to take effect.

Refinable: Yes - active ▼

Sortable:
Yes - active: Enables sorting the result set based
on the property before the result set is
returned. Use for example for large result sets
that cannot be sorted and retrieved at the same

Sortable: Yes - active ▼

For external content I usually select Include content from the first crawled property setting. These should be one-to-one mappings so it really doesn't make a difference. Click on the Add Mapping button:

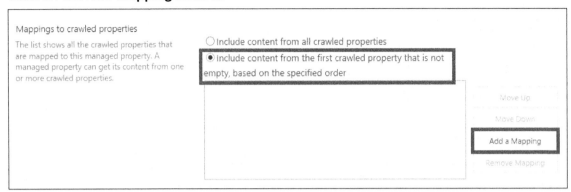

In the Crawled property dialog, select Business Data from the filter drop-down. Select the appropriate crawled property and click OK.

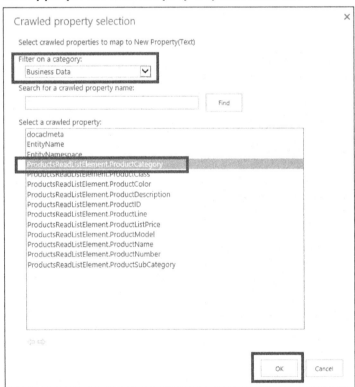

Back on the Add Managed Property page, click OK:

These managed properties are configured to be searchable, queryable, retrievable, sortable and refinable.

☐ Word Part Extraction - Custom5

☐ Word Exact Extraction - Custom

☐ Word Part Exact Extraction - Custom

OK   Cancel

You'll need to repeat this process for each crawled property.

Performing the mapping through the UI can become tedious. That's why I create a script to map all of my properties:

Add-PSSnapin Microsoft.SharePoint.PowerShell -ErrorAction SilentlyContinue

$ssa = Get-SPEnterpriseSearchServiceApplication

$crawledProperty = Get-SPEnterpriseSearchMetadataCrawledProperty -SearchApplication $ssa -Name ProductsReadListElement.ProductCategory

$managedProperty = New-SPEnterpriseSearchMetadataManagedProperty -SearchApplication $ssa -Name ProductCategory -FullTextQueriable:$true -Queryable:$true -Retrievable:$true -Type 1

New-SPEnterpriseSearchMetadataMapping -SearchApplication $ssa -ManagedProperty $managedProperty -CrawledProperty $crawledProperty

Just repeat the last three lines for each property mapping.

There are no parameters for sortable or refinable so I just go into the UI and change those settings manually for the properties I want to sort on or refine. You could create the crawled property if you knew what it was going to be named but in my script I get the crawled property since it was already created.

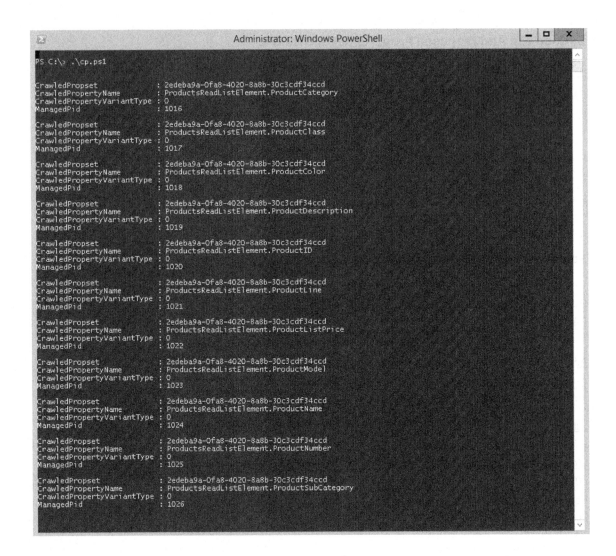

```
PS C:\> .\cp.ps1

CrawledPropset          : 2edeba9a-0fa8-4020-8a8b-30c3cdf34ccd
CrawledPropertyName     : ProductsReadListElement.ProductCategory
CrawledPropertyVariantType : 0
ManagedPid              : 1016

CrawledPropset          : 2edeba9a-0fa8-4020-8a8b-30c3cdf34ccd
CrawledPropertyName     : ProductsReadListElement.ProductClass
CrawledPropertyVariantType : 0
ManagedPid              : 1017

CrawledPropset          : 2edeba9a-0fa8-4020-8a8b-30c3cdf34ccd
CrawledPropertyName     : ProductsReadListElement.ProductColor
CrawledPropertyVariantType : 0
ManagedPid              : 1018

CrawledPropset          : 2edeba9a-0fa8-4020-8a8b-30c3cdf34ccd
CrawledPropertyName     : ProductsReadListElement.ProductDescription
CrawledPropertyVariantType : 0
ManagedPid              : 1019

CrawledPropset          : 2edeba9a-0fa8-4020-8a8b-30c3cdf34ccd
CrawledPropertyName     : ProductsReadListElement.ProductID
CrawledPropertyVariantType : 0
ManagedPid              : 1020

CrawledPropset          : 2edeba9a-0fa8-4020-8a8b-30c3cdf34ccd
CrawledPropertyName     : ProductsReadListElement.ProductLine
CrawledPropertyVariantType : 0
ManagedPid              : 1021

CrawledPropset          : 2edeba9a-0fa8-4020-8a8b-30c3cdf34ccd
CrawledPropertyName     : ProductsReadListElement.ProductListPrice
CrawledPropertyVariantType : 0
ManagedPid              : 1022

CrawledPropset          : 2edeba9a-0fa8-4020-8a8b-30c3cdf34ccd
CrawledPropertyName     : ProductsReadListElement.ProductModel
CrawledPropertyVariantType : 0
ManagedPid              : 1023

CrawledPropset          : 2edeba9a-0fa8-4020-8a8b-30c3cdf34ccd
CrawledPropertyName     : ProductsReadListElement.ProductName
CrawledPropertyVariantType : 0
ManagedPid              : 1024

CrawledPropset          : 2edeba9a-0fa8-4020-8a8b-30c3cdf34ccd
CrawledPropertyName     : ProductsReadListElement.ProductNumber
CrawledPropertyVariantType : 0
ManagedPid              : 1025

CrawledPropset          : 2edeba9a-0fa8-4020-8a8b-30c3cdf34ccd
CrawledPropertyName     : ProductsReadListElement.ProductSubCategory
CrawledPropertyVariantType : 0
ManagedPid              : 1026
```

In order for the Managed Properties to take effect, you now need to run a full crawl on the content source again.

Create a Result Source for the New Content Source

Navigate to your Search Center and select Site Settings from the Settings menu:

Under the Site Collection Administration section, click on Search Result Sources:

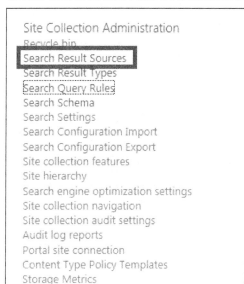

On the Manage Result Sources page, click on the New Result Source link:

Site Collection Administration › Manage Result Sources

Use result sources to scope search results and federate queries to external sources, such as internet search engines. After defining a
rule actions to use it. Learn more about result sources.

Result Sources replace Search Scopes, which are now deprecated. You can still view your old scopes and use them in queries, but n

≡ New Result Source

On the Add Result Source page, enter a name for the Result Source. For this example, I am using Products:

Search Center

Site Settings › Add Result Source

General Information

Names must be unique at each administrative level. For example, two result sources in a site
cannot share a name, but one in a site and one provided by the site collection can.

Descriptions are shown as tooltips when selecting result sources in other configuration
pages.

Name

Products   ✕

Description

Scroll down and click on the Launch Query Builder button:

In the Property Filter section, first select "--Show all managed properties--":

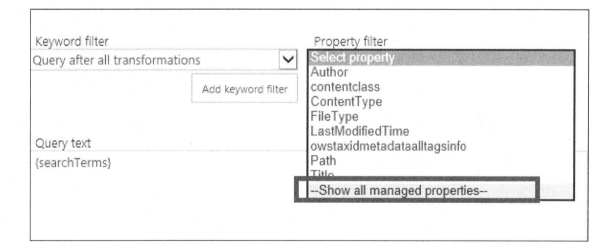

Next select ContentSource from the drop-down. Select Equals and Manual value:

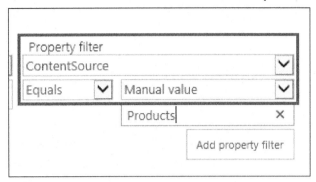

Enter the name of the content source (e.g. Products) in the text box and click Add property filter:

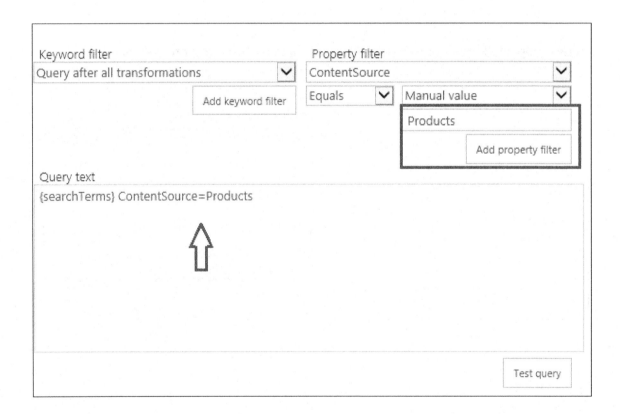

The property filter is added to the Query text.

Click OK on the Build Your Query dialog.

The property filter is added to the Query Transform text box.

Click Save:

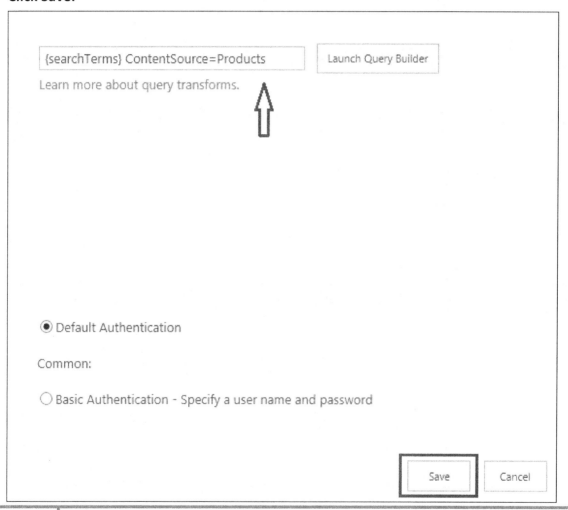

The new result source is created and appears under the Defined for this site section:

Search Center

Site Collection Administration

Use result sources to scope search results and federate queries to exter

Result Sources replace Search Scopes, which are now deprecated. You

🖼 New Result Source

    Name

Defined for this site collection (1)

    Products

Provided by SharePoint (16)

Create a Result Type for the Result Source

Navigate to your Search Center and select Site Settings from the Settings menu.

Under the Site Collection Administration section, click on the Search Result Types link:

Site Collection Administration
Recycle bin
Search Result Sources
Search Result Types
Search Query Rules
Search Schema
Search Settings
Search Configuration Import
Search Configuration Export
Site collection features
Site hierarchy
Search engine optimization settings
Site collection navigation

On the Result Types page click on the New Result Type link:

Search Center

Site Collection Administration

Tailor the look of important result types by crafting a display template in HTML and defining a rule tha priority. Learn more about how to configure result types.

New Result Type

Enter a name for the Result Type. Select the Result Source created in the previous section from the source drop-down. Skip the types of content rule. Select Default Item for now under "What should these results look like?". You will create a custom item template in later sections.

Search Center

Site Collection Administration › Add Result Type

apply to all sites in the site collection. To make one for just this site, use site result types.

Give it a name

Products

Which source should results match?

Products ▾

What types of content should match? You can skip this rule to match all content

Select a value ▾

Add value

What should these results look like?

Default Item ▾

Note: This result type will automatically update with the latest properties in your display template each time you visit the Manage Result Types Page.

Display template URL

~sitecollection/_catalogs/masterpage/Display Templates/Search/Item_Default.js

☐ Optimize for frequent use

Save   Cancel

Click Save.

Create a Search Results Page for the New Content Source

Navigate to your Search Center and select Site Contents from the Settings menu:

Locate and double-click the Pages library:

From the Files tab in the top ribbon, select Page from the New Document drop-down menu:

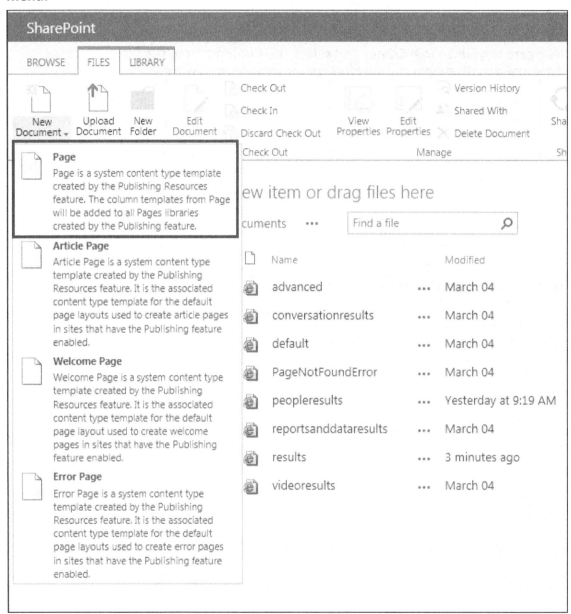

On the Create Page page, enter a title and URL Name. Click Create.

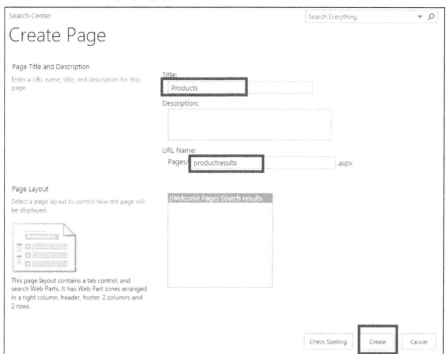

Select the ellipsis menu on the new page and click on OPEN:

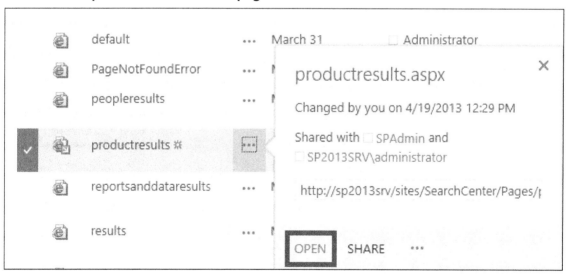

From the Settings menu select Edit page:

Locate the Search Results web part and select Edit Web Part from the drop-down menu:

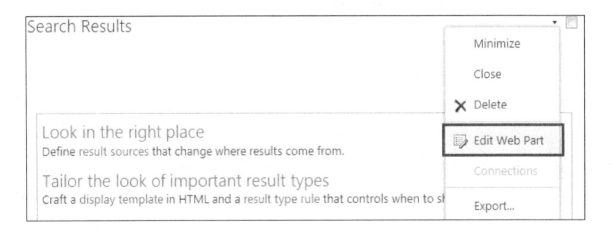

In the Properties tool pane that appeared on the right, click the Change query button:

The Build Your Query dialog appears.

In the Select a query section, select the custom Result Source created in the previous section of this chapter:

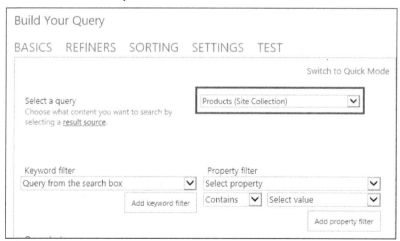

Click OK on the Build Your Query dialog.

Click OK in the web part properties tool pane:

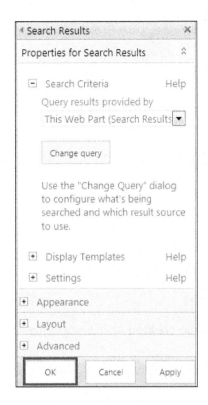

Check in the page:

Publish the page:

Add a Custom Results Page to the Search Center Navigation

Navigate to your Search Center and select Site Settings from the Settings menu:

Under the Search section click the Search Settings link:

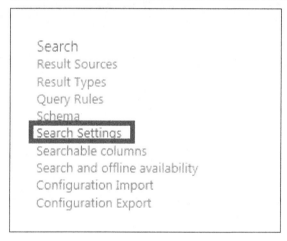

At the bottom the Search Settings page, click on Add Link...:

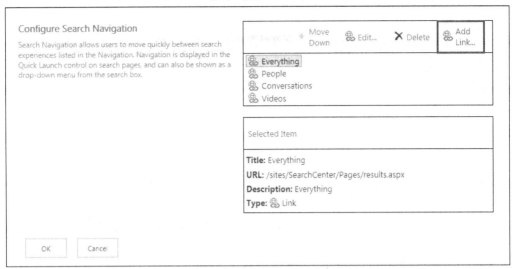

Enter a title and the URL to the custom page that was created in the previous section. Click OK.

Navigation Link   ✕

🗊   Edit the title, URL, and description of the navigation item.

Title: Products

URL: Center/Pages/productresults.aspx ✕   Browse...

☐ Open link in new window

Description:

Audience: 🕮 📇

Back on the Search Settings page click OK:

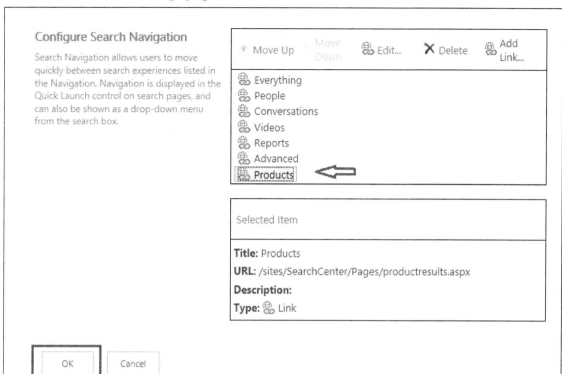

Test the Results

Navigate to your Search Center. The new navigation item appears at the top. Click on the new link and perform a search:

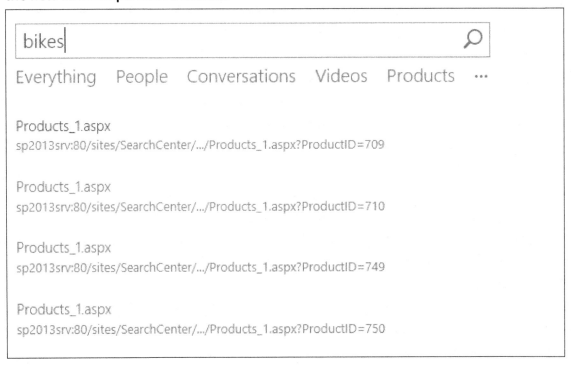

The results aren't too pretty. The next section explains how to create custom item templates and hover panels for the external content source.

Create an Item Display Template

Fire up SharePoint Designer 2013 and Open the Search Center Site:

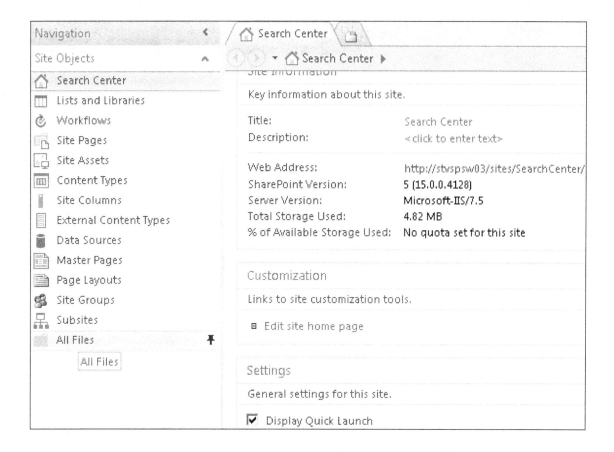

Click on All Files from the left-hand navigation:

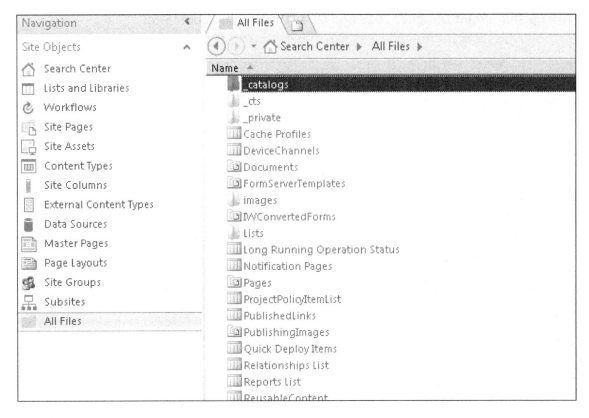

A list of all files is displayed in the main window.

If you attempt to get the files from the Master Pages object, you will not see any items once you get to the Display Templates folders.

Double-click on the _catalogs folder in the main window

This action displays the _catalogs structure under the left-hand navigation.

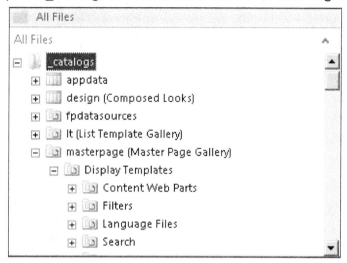

Expand the _catalogs folder, then the masterpage folder, and then the Display Templates folder.

Click on the Search folder under Display Templates:

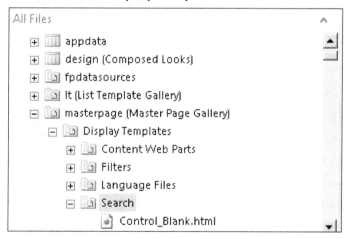

The list of Search display templates is shown in the main window area.

Locate Item_Default.html and Item_Default.js. Select both files, right-click, and select copy:

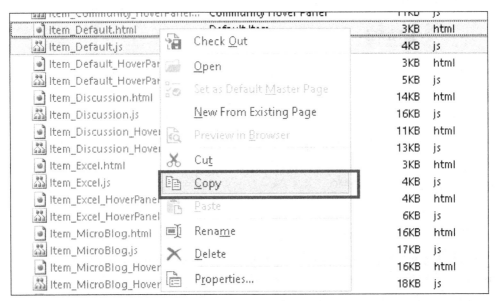

Right click again and select Paste:

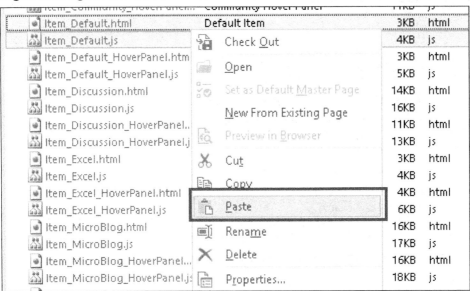

The files are copied in place.

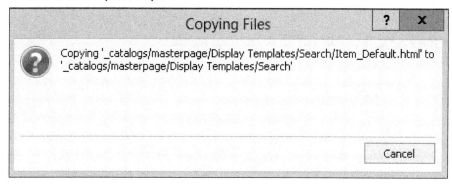

Rename the html copy:

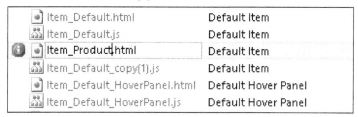

SharePoint automatically renames the .js file:

Item_PowerPoint_HoverPane...	PowerPoint Hover Panel	10KB	js
Item_Product.html	Default Item	3KB	html
Item_Product.js	Default Item	4KB	js
Item_Reply.html	Reply Item	14KB	html
Item_Reply.js	Reply Item	15KB	js

Right-click the html file and select Edit File in Advanced Mode:

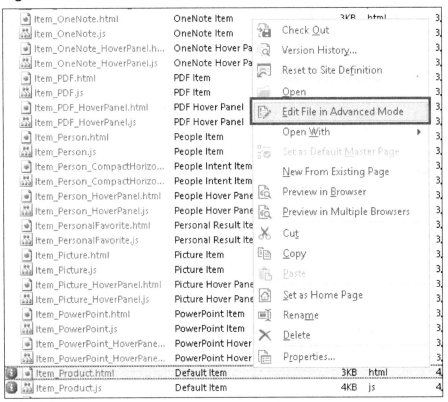

Rename the title:

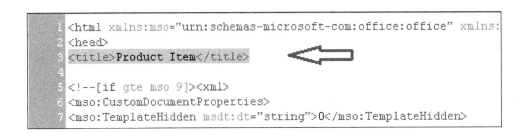

Add the external content type managed properties to the ManagedProperties tag:

```
<mso:ManagedPropertyMapping msdt:dt="string">&#39;ProductSubCategory&#39;:&#39;ProductSubCategory&#39;,&#39;ProductNumber&#39;:&#39;ProductNumber&#39;,&#39;
```

'ProductSubCategory':'ProductSubCategory','ProductNumber':'ProductNumber',

(see code examples on www.SteveTheManMann.com)

In the javascript code block, rename the hover panel:

```
if(!$isNull(ctx.CurrentItem) && !$isNull(ctx.ClientControl)){
    var id = ctx.ClientControl.get_nextUniqueId();
    var itemId = id + Srch.U.Ids.item;
    var hoverId = id + Srch.U.Ids.hover;
    var hoverUrl = "~sitecollection/_catalogs/masterpage/Display Templates/Search/Item_Product_HoverPanel.js";
    $setResultItem(itemId, ctx.CurrentItem);
    if(ctx.CurrentItem.IsContainer){
        ctx.CurrentItem.csr_Icon = Srch.U.getFolderIconUrl();
    }
    ctx.currentItem_ShowHoverPanelCallback = Srch.U.getShowHoverPanelCallback(itemId, hoverId, hoverUrl);
    ctx.currentItem_HideHoverPanelCallback = Srch.U.getHideHoverPanelCallback();
```

You will create the hover panel file in the next section.

Rename the data-displaytemplate:

```
<div id="_#= $htmlEncode(itemId) =#_" name="Item" data-displaytemplate="ProductItem" class=
    _#=ctx.RenderBody(ctx)=#_
    <div id="_#= $htmlEncode(hoverId) =#_" class="ms-srch-hover-outerContainer"></div>
</div>
```

In the javascript code block, I create variables that determine if there is data in the managed property fields:

```
<!--#_
     if(!$isNull(ctx.CurrentItem) && !$isNull(ctx.ClientControl)){
         var id = ctx.ClientControl.get_nextUniqueId();
         var itemId = id + Srch.U.Ids.item;
         var hoverId = id + Srch.U.Ids.hover;
         var hoverUrl = "~sitecollection/_catalogs/masterpage/Display Templates/Search/Item_Product_HoverPanel.js";
         $setResultItem(itemId, ctx.CurrentItem);
         if(ctx.CurrentItem.IsContainer){
             ctx.CurrentItem.csr_Icon = Srch.U.getFolderIconUrl();
         }

         var has_name = !$isEmptyString(ctx.CurrentItem.ProductName);
         var has_model = !$isEmptyString(ctx.CurrentItem.ProductModel);
         var has_number = !$isEmptyString(ctx.CurrentItem.ProductNumber);
         var has_category = !$isEmptyString(ctx.CurrentItem.ProductCategory);

         ctx.currentItem_ShowHoverPanelCallback = Srch.U.getShowHoverPanelCallback(itemId, hoverId, hoverUrl);
         ctx.currentItem_HideHoverPanelCallback = Srch.U.getHideHoverPanelCallback();
#-->
```

var has_name = !$isEmptyString(ctx.CurrentItem.ProductName);

var has_model = !$isEmptyString(ctx.CurrentItem.ProductModel);

var has_number = !$isEmptyString(ctx.CurrentItem.ProductNumber);

var has_category = !$isEmptyString(ctx.CurrentItem.ProductCategory);

Remove the ctx.RenderBody line:

```
         <div id="_#= $htmlEncode(itemId) =#_" name="It
             _#=ctx.RenderBody(ctx)=#_
             <div id="_#= $htmlEncode(hoverId) =#_" cl
         </div>
<!--#_
     }
#-->
```

For each managed property, create a code block similar to the following:

```
<!--#
        if(has_number == true) {
#-->
            <div id="ProductNumberField">
                <div id="ProductNumberValue" class="ms-srch-ellipsis" title="_#= ctx.CurrentItem.ProductNumber =#_">Product Number:  _#= ctx.CurrentItem.ProductNumber =#_ </div>
            </div>
<!--#
        }
#-->
```

<!--#

          if(has_number == true) {

 #-->

                  <div id="ProductNumberField">

                     <div id="ProductNumberValue" class="ms-srch-ellipsis" title="_#= ctx.CurrentItem.ProductNumber =#_ ">Product Number: #= ctx.CurrentItem.ProductNumber =#_ </div>

             </div>

<!--#

          }

 #-->

Code examples are available on www.SteveTheManMann.com.

```
<div id="_#= $htmlEncode(itemId) =#_ " name="Item" data-displaytemplate="ProductItem" class="ms-srch-item" onmouseover="_#= ctx.currentItem_ShowHoverPanelCallback =#_" onmouseout="_#=
        if(has_number == true) {
            <div id="ProductNumberField">
                <div id="ProductNumberValue" class="ms-srch-ellipsis" title="_#= ctx.CurrentItem.ProductNumber =#_">Product Number:  _#= ctx.CurrentItem.ProductNumber =#_ </div>
            </div>
        }

        if(has_name == true) {
            <div id="ProductNameField">
                <div id="ProductNameValue" class="ms-srch-ellipsis" title="_#= ctx.CurrentItem.ProductName =#_">Product Name:  _#= ctx.CurrentItem.ProductName =#_ </div>
            </div>
        }

        if(has_model == true) {
            <div id="ProductModelField">
                <div id="ProductModelValue" class="ms-srch-ellipsis" title="_#= ctx.CurrentItem.ProductModel =#_">Product Model:  _#= ctx.CurrentItem.ProductModel =#_ </div>
            </div>
        }
```

Save the html file.

Create an Item Hover Panel

Back in the listing of display templates, locate and select the Item_Default_HoverPanel files.

Right-click and select Copy:

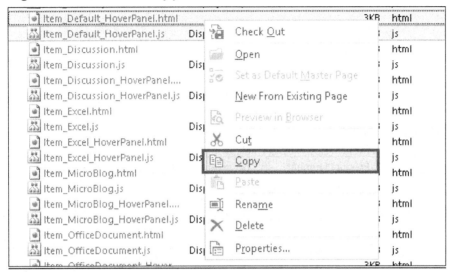

Right-click again and select Paste:

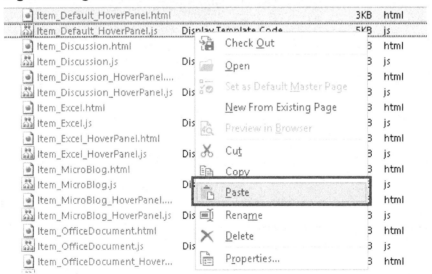

Rename the html file:

SharePoint automatically renames the .js file:

Item_Product.html	Item Display Template
Item_Product.js	Display Template Code
Item_Product_HoverPanel.html	Item Display Template
Item_Product_HoverPanel.js	Display Template Code

Right click the html file and select Edit File in Advanced Mode:

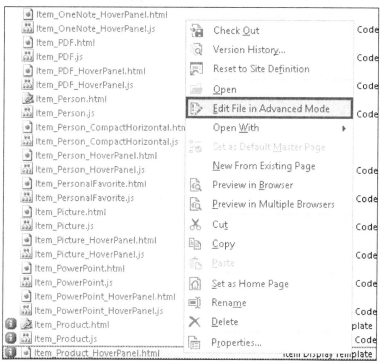

Rename the title:

```
1 <html xmlns:mso="urn:schemas-microsoft-com:office:office"
2 <head>
3 <title>Product Hover Panel</title>
4
5 <!--[if gte mso 9]><xml>
6 <mso:CustomDocumentProperties>
```

Copy and paste the ManagedPropertyMapping from the item display template created in the previous section:

```
5 <!--[if gte mso 9]><xml>
6 <mso:CustomDocumentProperties>
7 <mso:TemplateHidden msdt:dt="string">0</mso:TemplateHidden>
8 <mso:MasterPageDescription msdt:dt="string">Displays the default hover panel template.</mso:MasterPageDescription>
9 <mso:ContentTypeId msdt:dt="string">0x0101002039C03B61C64EC4A04F5361F385106603</mso:ContentTypeId>
10 <mso:TargetControlType msdt:dt="string">;#SearchHoverPanel;#</mso:TargetControlType>
11 <mso:HtmlDesignAssociated msdt:dt="string">1</mso:HtmlDesignAssociated>
12 <mso:ManagedPropertyMapping msdt:dt="string">&#39;ProductSubCategory&#39;:&#39;ProductSubCategory&#39;,&#39;ProductNumber&#39;:&#39;P
13 &#39;Title&#39;:&#39;Title&#39;,&#39;Path&#39;:&#39;Path&#39;,&#39;Description&#39;:&#39;Description&#39;,&#39;EditorOWSUSER&#39;:&
14 <mso:HtmlDesignConversionSucceeded msdt:dt="string">True</mso:HtmlDesignConversionSucceeded>
15 <mso:HtmlDesignStatusAndPreview msdt:dt="string">http://sp2013srv/sites/SearchCenter/_catalogs/masterpage/Display%20Templates/Search/
16 </mso:CustomDocumentProperties>
```

Rename the Default entries:

```
<body>
    <div id="Item Product HoverPanel">
<!--#
    var i = 0;
    var id = ctx.CurrentItem.csr_id;
    ctx.CurrentItem.csr_ShowViewLibrary = !Srch.U.isWebPage(ctx.CurrentItem.FileExtension);
    if(ctx.CurrentItem.IsContainer)
    {
        ctx.CurrentItem.csr_FileType = Srch.Res.ct_Folder
    }

    ctx.currentItem_ShowChangedBySnippet = true;

_#-->
    <div class="ms-srch-hover-innerContainer ms-srch-hover-standardSize" id="_#= $htmlEncode(id + HP.ids.inner) =#_">
        <div class="ms-srch-hover-arrowBorder" id="_#= $htmlEncode(id + HP.ids.arrowBorder) =#_"></div>
        <div class="ms-srch-hover-arrow" id="_#= $htmlEncode(id + HP.ids.arrow) =#_"></div>
        <div class="ms-srch-hover-content" id="_#= $htmlEncode(id + HP.ids.content) =#_" data-displaytemplate="ProductHoverPanel">
            <div id="_#= $htmlEncode(id + HP.ids.header) =#_" class="ms-srch-hover-header">
                _#= ctx.RenderHeader(ctx) =#_
```

Create variables for the managed properties you wish to display in the hover panel:

```
var has_name = !$isEmptyString(ctx.CurrentItem.ProductName);
var has_description = !$isEmptyString(ctx.CurrentItem.ProductDescription);
var has_color = !$isEmptyString(ctx.CurrentItem.ProductColor);
var has_listprice = !$isEmptyString(ctx.CurrentItem.ProductListPrice);
var has_category = !$isEmptyString(ctx.CurrentItem.ProductCategory);
var has_subcategory = !$isEmptyString(ctx.CurrentItem.ProductSubCategory);
```

Remove the Render Header <div>:

```
<div class="ms-srch-hover-content" id="_#= $htmlEncode(id + HP.ids.content) =#_" data-displaytemplate="ProductHoverPanel">
    <div id="_#= $htmlEncode(id + HP.ids.header) =#_" class="ms-srch-hover-header">
        _#= ctx.RenderHeader(ctx) =#_
    </div>
    <div id="_#= $htmlEncode(id + HP.ids.body) =#_" class="ms-srch-hover-body">
<!--#_
```

Remove the ctx.RenderBody line:

```
<div class="ms-srch-hover-innerContainer ms-srch-hover-star
    <div class="ms-srch-hover-arrowBorder" id="_#= $htmlEnc
    <div class="ms-srch-hover-arrow" id="_#= $htmlEncode(id
    <div class="ms-srch-hover-content" id="_#= $htmlEncode
        <div id="_#= $htmlEncode(id + HP.ids.header) =#_"
            _#= ctx.RenderHeader(ctx) =#_
        </div>
        <div id="_#= $htmlEncode(id + HP.ids.body) =#_" cl
            _#= ctx.RenderBody(ctx) =#_
        </div>
        <div id="_#= $htmlEncode(id + HP.ids.actions) =#_"
            _#= ctx.RenderFooter(ctx) =#_
        </div>
    </div>
</div>
```

Again, add code blocks for each managed property. Example files are located on www.SteveTheManMann.com:

```
<div id="_#= $htmlEncode(id + HP.ids.body) =#_" class="ms-srch-hover-body">

    if(has_name == true) {

        <div id="ProductNameField">
            <div id="ProductNameValue" class="ms-srch-ellipsis" style="font-weight:bold"
        </div>

    }


    if(has_description == true) {

        <div id="ProductDescriptionField">
            <div id="ProductDescriptionValue" class="ms-srch-ellipsis" title="_#= ctx.Cur
        </div>

    }


    if(has_color == true) {

        <div id="ProductColorField">
            <div id="ProductColorValue" class="ms-srch-ellipsis" title="_#= ctx.CurrentI
        </div>

    }
```

Save the file.

Update the Result Type to Use the New Display Template

Navigate to your Search Center and select Site Settings from the Settings menu.

Under the Site Collection Administration section, click on the Search Result Types link:

Locate the external content type Result Type and select Edit from the drop-down menu:

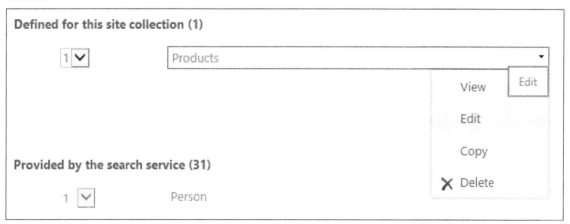

Change the What should these results look like? to the new display template created in the previous sections:

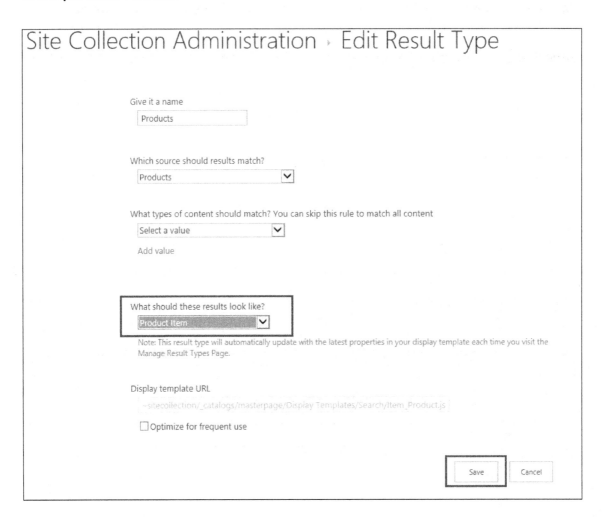

Click Save.

Test the Item Display Template and Hover Panel

Navigate to your Search Center and perform a search within the new results page:

Product Number: SO-B909-M
Product Name: Mountain Bike Socks, M
Product Model: Mountain Bike Socks
Product Category: Clothing

Product Number: SO-B909-L
Product Name: Mountain Bike Socks, L
Product Model: Mountain Bike Socks
Product Category: Clothing

Product Number: BK-R93R-62
Product Name: Road-150 Red, 62
Product Model: Road-150
Product Category: Bikes

Product Number: BK-R93R-44
Product Name: Road-150 Red, 44
Product Model: Road-150
Product Category: Bikes

Product Number: BK-R93R-48
Product Name: Road-150 Red, 48
Product Model: Road-150
Product Category: Bikes

Road-150 Red, 62
This bike is ridden by race winners. Developed with the
Adventure Works Cycles professional race team, it has a
extremely light heat-treated aluminum frame, and steering
that allows precision control.

Color: Red
List Price: 3578.27
Product Category: Bikes
Product SubCategory: Road Bikes

OPEN   SEND

The results are shown with the managed property values and the hover panel displays additional information.

Add Custom Sort Options

Now that you have results from your external content type, it would be nice if the user could sort their search results based on some of the managed properties that are now available. Properties used for sorting must be configured as Sortable.

Navigate to the custom results page that was created for the external content type and use the Settings menu to edit the page:

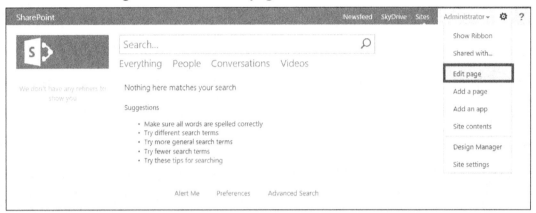

Select Edit Web Part from the Search Results drop-down menu:

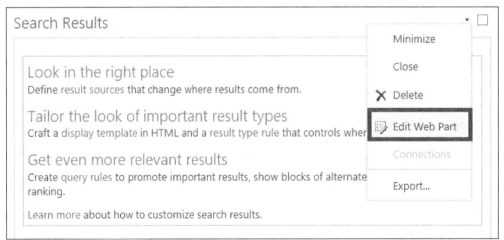

The Search Results web part properties pane is displayed on the right of the page.

Expand the Settings section and check the Show sort dropdown box:

Copy the JSON from the text box underneath and paste it within a text editor:

```
Untitled - Notepad
File  Edit  Format  View  Help
[{"name":"Relevance","sorts":[]},{"name":"Date(Newest)","sorts":[{"p":"Write","d":1}]},
{"name":"Date(Oldest)","sorts":[{"p":"Write","d":0}]},
{"name":"Lifetime Views","sorts":[{"p":"ViewsLifeTime","d":1}]},
{"name":"Recent Views","sorts":[{"p":"ViewsRecent","d":1}]}]
```

Line breaks were entered for presentation purposes.

For this example, I removed the Date sorts and replaced them with Category and Color:

```
Untitled - Notepad
File  Edit  Format  View  Help
[{"name":"Relevance","sorts":[]},
{"name":"Category","sorts":[{"p":"ProductCategory","d":0}]},
{"name":"Color","sorts":[{"p":"ProductColor","d":0}]},
{"name":"Lifetime Views","sorts":[{"p":"ViewsLifeTime","d":1}]},
{"name":"Recent Views","sorts":[{"p":"ViewsRecent","d":1}]}]
```

[{"name":"Relevance","sorts":[]},

{"name":"Category","sorts":[{"p":"ProductCategory","d":0}]},

{"name":"Color","sorts":[{"p":"ProductColor","d":0}]},

{"name":"Lifetime Views","sorts":[{"p":"ViewsLifeTime","d":1}]},

{"name":"Recent Views","sorts":[{"p":"ViewsRecent","d":1}]}]

Copy and Paste the modifications back into the text box within the web part properties. Click OK on the web part properties pane.

Check in the page:

⚠ **Checked out to you** Only you can see your recent changes. Check it in.

Publish the page:

⚠ **Recent draft not published** Visitors can't see recent changes. Publish this draft.

The Search Results page now displays a sort drop-down at the top of the page:

Selecting a sort option displays the search results sorted by the selected property:

Add Custom Refinements

You may also use the managed properties to provide the user options in refining the search results. Properties used for refinement must be configured as Refinable.

Navigate to the custom results page that was created for the external content type and use the Settings menu to edit the page:

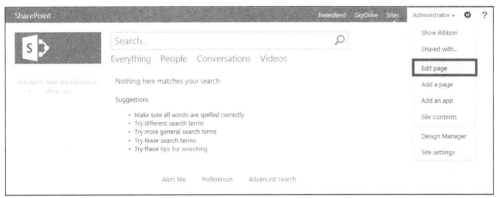

Select Edit Web Part from the Refinement drop-down menu:

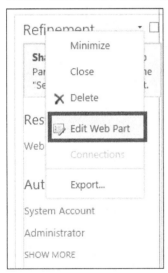

The Refinement web part properties pane is displayed on the right of the page.

The main option in this web part is to configure the refiners for the search results of the given page by clicking the Choose Refiners...button:

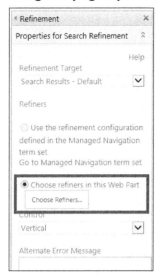

The Refinement configuration dialog appears:

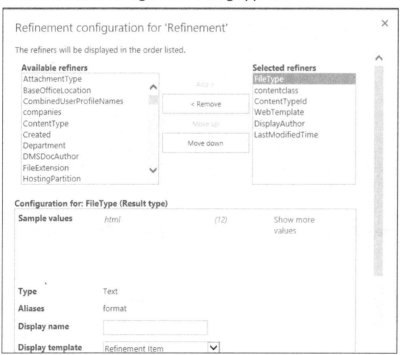

For this example, I do not need the out-of-the-box default refiners. So I selected each property from the Selected refiners box and click the Remove button to remove each one:

Scroll down the Available refiners and locate external content type properties that have been configured as Refinable:

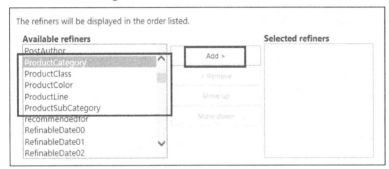

Notice it was a good idea to include the entity as a prefix of each managed property as they are all grouped together and easily locatable.

Select each one and click the Add button to add each property as a Selected refiner.

Use the Move up and/or the Move down buttons to re-order the selected refiners:

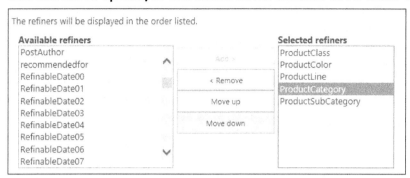

Select each property and enter a Display name, Sort by, and Sort direction:

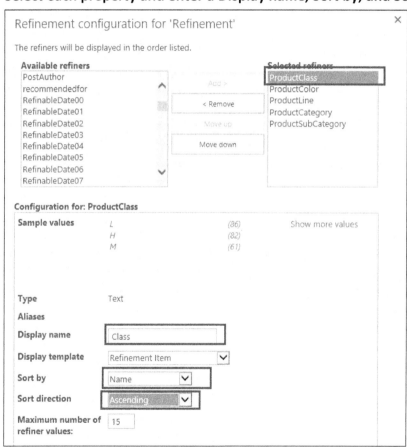

Once completed, click OK on the Refinement dialog:

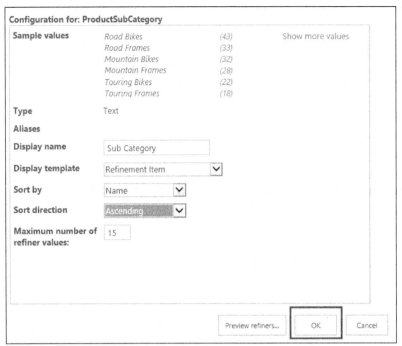

Don't forget to click OK in the Refinement web part properties:

Check in the page:

Publish the page:

Perform a search. The custom refinements appear on the left-hand side of the results page:

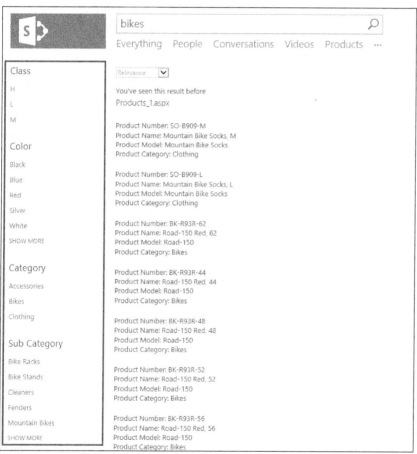

THIS PAGE INTENTIONALLY BLANK

Modifying Search Display Templates

This appendix outlines the initial steps needed to modify the Display Templates used in Search using SharePoint Designer 2013. Many of the customizations in this book deal with modifying (or copying and modifying) the Display Templates. Here is how you get to them.

Step 1: Fire up SharePoint Designer 2013 and Open the Search Center Site

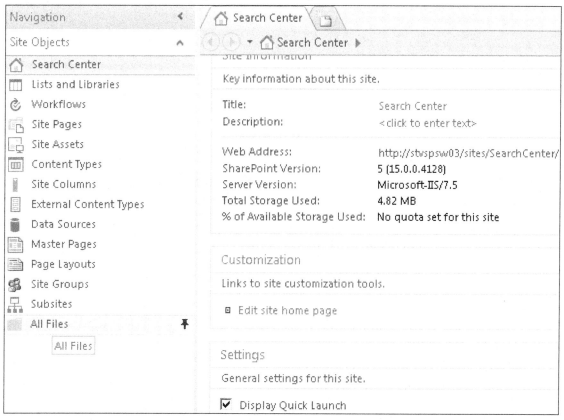

Step 2: Click on All Files from the left-hand navigation

If you attempt to get the files from the Master Pages, you will not see any items once you get to the Display Templates folders.

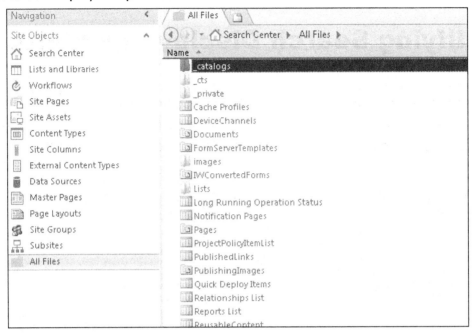

You see the list of all files in the main window.

Step 3: Double-click on the _catalogs folder in the main window

This action displays the _catalogs structure under the left-hand navigation.

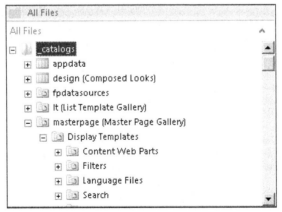

Expand the _catalogs folder, then the masterpage folder, and then the Display Templates folder.

Step 4: Click on the Search folder under Display Templates

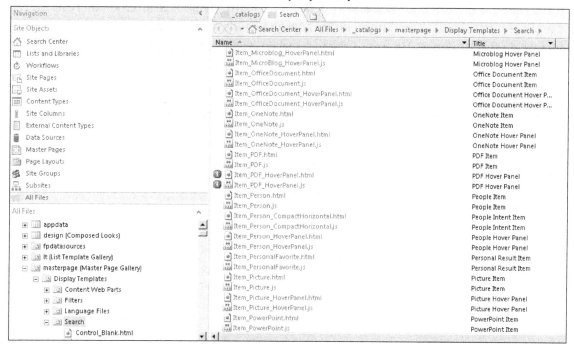

While most of the templates modified in this book appear under the Search folder, several appear under the Filters folder.

About the Author

Steve Mann was born and raised in Philadelphia, Pennsylvania, where he still resides. He is an Enterprise Application Engineer for Morgan Lewis and has more than 19 years of professional experience. He has authored and co-authored several books related to collaboration technology. Steve graduated Drexel University in 1993.

Steve's blog site can be found at: www.SteveTheManMann.com

Follow Steve on Twitter @stevethemanmann

CPSIA information can be obtained
at www.ICGtesting.com
Printed in the USA
FSOW04n2150270916
25492FS